OPERATION
Military Family

*How To Strengthen Your Military
Marriage and Save Your Family*

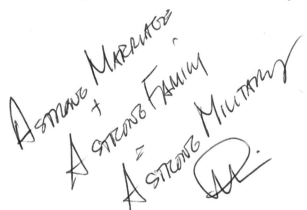

MICHAEL J.R. SCHINDLER

AVIVA
PUBLISHING

NEW YORK

Operation Military Family:
How to Strengthen Your Military Marriage and Save Your Family

Operation Military Family
23632 Hwy 99, Ste F #354
Edmonds, WA 98026
info@operationmilitaryfamily.org

ISBN 10: 1-890427-86-1
ISBN 13: 978-1-890427-86-3

Library of Congress #: 2007939754

Publisher: Aviva Publishing, Lake Placid, NY
Editor: Shannon Evans
Cover Design: Jeff Hinckle, Shoto Design

Every attempt has been made to properly source all quotes.

Printed in the United States of America

First Edition

For additional copies of this book, please visit www.operationmilitary family.org. A portion of all proceeds from the sale of books is directed toward programs and events designed to strengthen and empower military couples and their marriages.

"Never in the history of the United States has the senior military leadership paid more attention to families, including the saving and strengthening of military marriages. Operation Military Family will serve as a great tool, in support of these efforts, for the dedicated families of our military, all being stretched by the challenges of multiple deployments and frequent moves. Whether active duty, National Guard or Reserve, the family issues are similar and this book should be a ready resource for all. I will be recommending it to military families, commanders, chaplains, civilian religious leaders and anyone interested in supporting our great military families!"

– Chaplain (Colonel) Mack Griffith
United States Army Reserve Command

Acclaim for
Operation Military Family:
How to Strengthen Your Military
Marriage and Save Your Family

"In December of 1991, while I was deployed onboard the submarine USS James Madison, a man dressed as a Christmas elf pulled up outside my house. Imagine the look on my young children's faces – and their mother's – as he gave my children a small gift and wished them a merry Christmas. That young man was Mike Schindler.

This book is a testament to Mike's lifelong commitment to caring for our military and their families. Mike has taken this calling and put together the most comprehensive and valuable resource for military families that I have seen in 20 years of active duty service. This book is as essential to military families as boots are to a soldier, and should be required reading for all."

– SCPO Mark Campbell, United States Navy

* * * * *

"As a military mother, I value what Mike Schindler is doing to encourage and strengthen our military families. As our Army Reserves son and his bride begin their life together, they accept the possibilities of what military service may bring their way. May they stay strong, encouraged, and grow as one. I cannot wait to share Mike's book with them!"

– Lucy A. Cain, Author
Secure the Fort (And Remain Under God),
A Military Mother's Message to America
2007 Gold Medal Award for Best Anthology,
Military Writers Society of America

* * * * *

"Both the length and depth of the material seem so very practical because people will be able to read it quickly but they will also find answers that satisfy their questions. I expect to be using it for a lot of soldiers."

– CH (MAJ) Kenneth L. Alford
1st Joint Mobilization Brigade Chaplain
Four Chaplains Memorial Chapel (4CMC) OIC

* * * * *

"Author and military marriage advocate, Mike Schindler, has written a must read road map to strengthen the marriages of our courageous military families. He is passionate yet brings compassion to military marriages because he has been there. This resource needs to be in the homes and hearts of every military marriage in America. Spread the word...Mike Schindler is offering hope to our military marriages."

– Dr. Gary and Barb Rosberg
America's Family Coaches, Speakers,
Authors of *6 Secrets to a Lasting Love*,
and grateful citizens

* * * * *

"The stress of military deployment particularly for service members in the National Guard and Reserve can paralyze a family. When the time between activation notice and actual deployment is compressed, it is critical that families have a guide to keep them focused. Operation Military Family is a resource that makes deployment preparation and return easier."

– Lourdes E. Alvarado-Ramos (Alfie)
Deputy Director, WA Department of Veterans Affairs

* * * * *

"This book will save military marriages and prevent children from growing up in broken families.

Send a copy of this book to our soldiers and provide hope during times of unthinkable adversities."

– Patrick Snow, Best-Selling Author of
Creating Your Own Destiny

* * * * *

"After reading Operation Military Family I felt encouraged and challenged. As a family therapist in an area with multiple military bases I commonly see families who have been affected by the recent wars/conflicts. While in my doctoral program a very wise professor told me that life is made up of a series of attachments and separations. This is never more true than for military family members. For those families in need of direction I have a new tool that is a valuable resource for dealing correctly with these transitions. I also sensed in the book Mike's deep compassion and commitment for military families. It stirred my heart for hurting families who have been touched in a way that many of us who have not served in the military (myself included) will only know from a distance. This book will help me better understand their journey. I am grateful to Mike for allowing me the opportunity to be a small part of this undertaking. I am indeed honored."

– Kenneth A. Ackerman, Ph.D., LMFT
Licensed Marriage & Family Therapist

Dedication

I am truly passionate about my family – or what I commonly refer to as "my girls." They inspire me and most days I realize how blessed I am to have them in my life.

I am also extremely passionate about the freedoms we have in this country. Every day there are men and women who dedicate their lives ensuring those freedoms are protected. They live by a different set of rules and laws, often sacrificing their freedoms so that I can experience mine. I am forever grateful.

To "my girls" and to the men and women who guard our freedom, I dedicate this book.

Contents

Acknowledgements

I want to thank my wife, Keri, for her involvement and her insight in many of the interviews. She often brought the feeling into what I would have treated as 'just another interview'. She gave me the often needed encouragement to push forward and finish. I admire her patience with me through this process.

I am most grateful to my publishing coach, Patrick Snow, for his guidance. As a best selling author, he was familiar with the journey and some of the short cuts that made writing and finishing this book in a relatively short period of time possible.

Shannon Evans, my editor, is a God-send. Her personal experiences and involvement with our Armed Forces, as well as her perspective, brought a balance to my writing. She is a wealth of knowledge and support and I am quite thankful for her commitment to this project.

Jeff Hinckle, with Shoto Design, who devoted countless hours to perfecting the covers, I thank you. I wanted to convey an image of vulnerability and strength and Jeff took my conflicted ideas and managed to pull together, in my opinion, a masterpiece.

I especially want to thank all the military couples, chaplains, counselors and administrators who selflessly gave of their time, shared their knowledge and opened up their lives so that others could learn from their experiences. It is because of their selflessness that our country remains great. My family and I will be forever grateful for their service to our country.

Most importantly, I wish to honor and thank God for planting the seed from which this book grew. This was a true test of faith for me.

Preface

Pay attention. The family unit is endangered. Whether you are serving in the military or know someone who is serving, this issue affects you. The government knows it and is fighting like hell to preserve families, despite what the media portrays. If marriages, especially military marriages, continue to suffer, our armed forces will be weak and our country will not only suffer but will become extremely vulnerable.

When I set out on this project, my initial thoughts were to compile all the emails, thoughts, letters and pictures I received from the Afghan front into a personal book – a keepsake about the experience my best friend, Brian and his family, walked through while he was in Afghanistan. My plan was to call it the Forgotten War: letters from the Afghan Front and present it to Brian as a keepsake…no one would know I borrowed the title often given to the Korean War.

But then I realized, through all the back and forth emails and instant messages, there is a whole new war that truly has been forgotten…or maybe just ignored. It is a war that the government is aggressively fighting to win but receives little to no coverage for their efforts. This war has already had a devastating effect on our communities, our children and our nation and will continue to do so if we don't win the fight; and that is the fight to keep military families together, both during and after the war.

My passion for this issue stems from my own military background and my personal experience with having divorced parents. My mom and dad grew up in the "My Three Sons" generation. I grew up in the "my three dads" era. The simple fact is the divorce rate in the US is high regardless of whether one serves or not; but when one couples that with the stress and demands of being called to war, or readjustment back to "normal" life after the war, divorce among military families skyrockets. Some will point to the newly released RAND study, conducted by the National Defense Research Institute, that suggests improvements in reducing the divorce rate among military families have been made. No question, there have been improvements.

But research conducted by the Department of Defense still shows that approximately 20 percent of marriages fall apart within two years when one spouse has been sent off to war. And if you're an officer your chances of getting a divorce has climbed 78 percent since 2001. Why so high for officers? There are several schools of thought on this, but the most widely perceived reason is because both spouses are typically college educated, have professional careers, and deployment was never considered as a true factor in the marriage. And when deployment comes into the picture, the spouse left behind has no interest in accepting a long distance relationship – it doesn't fit with the original and professional vision.

As reported by Divorce Magazine, the average divorce rate of the general US population is 36 percent. The negative impact of the increased number of divorces among military families will have a negative impact on future generations of our nation.

A research brief conducted by the Center for Marriage and Families reports that divorce doubles the risk that children will experience serious psychological problems. It increases the risk of depression in children... and because of this, the suicide rate among teens and young adults has reportedly tripled in the last fifty years. According to a Swedish study, as adults, children raised in single-parent families were 56 percent more likely to show signs of mental illness than children from intact married homes. Forty years ago, according to divorcereform.org, 90 percent of children were reared to maturity by their married, natural parents. Today, that figure is 68 percent. More than one in four children are living in a sole-parent family or step/blended family from which one natural parent is absent, nearly always the natural father. Imagine that. And we question what's wrong with our children?

Maybe you're thinking 'hey we don't have kids; if we got divorced, the effects wouldn't be felt.' Think again. One of the most authoritative studies conducted in the United States on mental health found that those who divorce are nearly twice as likely to suffer from mental illness as those who are married. Still think divorce is the answer? Expect an increase in depression, poor work performance—

especially in men and a likely increase in alcohol abuse. In most cases, remarriage does not improve your psychological well-being, except of course in the case of violent or abusive relationships.

So where do you go from here? That honeymoon feeling of absolute excitement is gone, your marriage is not what you expected it to be, you are under the stress of bills, deadlines, demands, your emotions are rocked, dating your spouse disappeared when the kids showed up, and the only dreams you have left are the ones you see with your eyes closed. And now even those are replaced by the nightmare of war. You feel like a stranger in your own family…and divorce truly just is not an option.

First, know that you are not alone and there is hope. The military is treating this issue very seriously and has made it a top priority to support and reconnect couples as part of the military experience. There are a number of services made available by the government to help military families work on saving their marriages and you will discover some of those in this book. Some of these programs have not been showcased in the media, and the unfortunate part is that many families, especially Reservists, just do not know where to look. If you are like most people, your research starts on Google, and as of this writing, when you do a simple Google search for military families, the information is decentralized at best and most likely buried under multiple links. The resources highlighted in this book will hopefully simplify and expedite your search.

The greatest benefits you will derive from this book are the strategies, lessons and tips you will learn from military families who have been right where you are. They will share their personal stories of how they successfully maintained, and continue to grow their marriages despite all the issues associated with war time service.

These families share from the heart…and the stories are very personal. What you'll learn is very powerful. They share how they fought loneliness, how they dealt with going from civilian life to "military family," the issues surrounding separation and single parenting and how they kept their spouse in the picture despite the distance. They survived. They took steps to remain "sane" when they had no communication with their loved one for days and months; and most importantly, they learned to live with each other after the war experience. Every day they work to win the fight to keep their marriages and their families together.

This is not, unfortunately, a cure-all. By the time you finish this book, you will have gained hope, you will understand that there are resources available to you and that there is no shame in seeking counseling – or coaching. The true part in overcoming any marital challenges caused by deployment is to first realize it is a family effort, not just an individual effort. Divorce is not part of overcoming. War is tragic, no question…but it does not have to claim your family.

Introduction

America and her people changed forever on September 11, 2001. We felt vulnerable, scared, enraged, and 100 percent patriotic. Terrorists struck at our core sense of security in a way we never imagined. Most of us were so consumed with our own drama that we didn't realize there was a problem...until that day. "Why" seemed to be the question that echoed throughout the country; but it was quickly exchanged for a "with us or against us" attitude.

We awakened and became a unified, passionate nation once again. The nation as a whole rallied behind President Bush when he declared to a rapt TV audience, "A great people have been moved to defend a great nation." Those simple provocative words rang true in the hearts of millions. The result was a marked increase in the number of people expressing interest in the armed forces. Men and women rushed to enlist and we, as a nation, were ready to fight.

But did we understand what the fight was or who we were actually fighting? Did we even begin to fathom how this "fight" would affect our families? Did we truly understand that it would be our brothers, sisters, moms, dads, uncles, aunts, husbands, wives, sons, daughters, and our best friends that would be doing the fighting? We wanted revenge, but not at the expense of our loved ones. We wanted to fight as long as no one got hurt. We wanted to serve but did we understand the effects and consequences that service would have on our families?

Every war has its brutal stories, its amazing heroes, and its hated villains. This war is no different. Death, injuries and unknown symptoms have been widely reported, as in previous wars. We have been introduced to the stories from the frontlines, we have met many heroes and we know the villains. But there has been little attention given to what the military is doing to reconnect couples and combat the negative effects war has on the military family. Since 2001, over 1.5 million Americans have served or are serving in the Iraq and Afghanistan War. There has been a perceived substantial increase in divorce throughout the enlisted and officer ranks and the military recognizes that as this perception grows, they lose families, and they lose recruits.

This book sheds light on the importance the military is placing on strengthening military marriages in an effort to reverse the perception. This book is also about overcoming and fighting against the struggles and issues brought on by deployment. It won't be easy. But nobody promised easy. What I will promise you is that you'll gain from other people's experiences, and should you choose to implement, this can mean the difference between divorce and a marriage that is worth the fight.

And know this, what you are about to read is raw and filled with truth. Nothing is fictionalized. These are the thoughts, feelings and experiences of soldiers who served either on the battlefield or in various support roles away from home as well as the thoughts and feelings of their families serving with them back at the home front. All of the soldiers interviewed believed it was their duty to deploy and fight. Most of the family members recognized this as well. What most did not realize was that they would have to fight to keep their families together. This is their journey.

CHAPTER 1

Why Do We Join?

Why do we join? Especially now? To join the military now, most Americans clearly understand that it is not a matter of if he or she gets activated and deployed, but *when*. If you are single, all you have to do is convince yourself your decision to join is a good one. But if you are married, there are many issues that affect not only you but your spouse, and any children you may have running around your home. Yet, single or married, we still join. Our nation currently has over 400,000 Americans serving in the military Reserve and Guard, many of them activated and joining the over 1.4 million others that have chosen to make one of the services their career. And though the media may report that some monthly military quotas aren't met, the year to year facts are clear: overall, excluding the Air Force and Navy, there are more men and women serving in the Armed Forces in 2007 than there were in 2006. So why *do* Americans continue to join, and more importantly, what factors should you consider before joining or continuing your service?

There are many different answers to these questions so we'll explore just a few. Perhaps these answers will help you solidify your choice as you get ready to embark on one the greatest, yet likely most difficult, journeys in your life.

Making a Difference

For some, the military is a last resort. To most, the reason to join involves a combination of factors like family tradition, patriotism, benefits and the absolute hip, exciting, adventure that is advertised.

According to the U.S. General Accounting Office, the military's recruitment advertising budget doubled from $300 million to nearly $600 million between 1998 and 2003. In 2004, the overall recruiting budget approached $4 billion. To attract the best, it costs money.

I personally was enamored by the professional recruiting ads. The government spends billions to create a very positive image. Young adults, fresh out of high school see the military as a great place to start adulthood. For many who have tasted corporate life and have felt that empty or dissatisfied, lack of making a difference feeling, there is often a belief that a military career will fill that void. We all want to know that what we are doing with our lives is making a difference. The military understands this need so they highlight the adventure, brotherhood, action-packed days, helicopter rides, education and patriotism. Discipline, leadership skills, and team work are all part of the recruiting package as well. As a result, the military is able to attract many talented men and women from all walks of life. And that attraction often starts with the advertising.

But for those who joined after September 11, 2001, the reason to join and continue to serve often starts with a feeling of patriotism and goes much deeper than advertising.

Mike's Story – The Need to Serve

The reasons to enlist in the service are historically vast, but for those who have joined recently, the reason is simple: you want to make a difference. And those who make a difference do so by serving a great cause. Mike was a perfect example of someone who wanted to make a difference. He felt something was missing until he joined the Army Reserves.

I couldn't wait to meet Mike. My wife knew Tonia, Mike's wife, and spoke highly of Tonia's resolve and strength throughout Mike's tour in Iraq. As a result, I was *certain* Mike was one of the few who had communicated extensively with his family his purpose and goal for needing to join the Reserves. Of course in my mind, it was Mike's clear explanation that caused Tonia to find her strength and comfort (is there truly such a thing?) throughout his tour because she knew the "why." Well, it wasn't exactly as I thought.

When I sat down with Mike and Tonia, they shared the "real" story. Mike changed Tonia's life quite unexpectedly on April 1, 2003. Now there are times throughout life when we all make what we think is a major decision, only to forget we made it three days later. And then there are times when our loved one makes a major decision that we never forget, and for better or for worse, *requires* us to work through that decision together. This was one of *those* times for Mike and Tonia. Pregnant with their second child, Tonia was not humored by Mike's decision to come home from work with reenlistment papers. Living what she considered a "normal" life for the past eight years of their marriage, the last thing she wanted to become was a military wife. Mike had served before in the Marines and had even spent time in Somalia. She had heard some of the stories from that experience and wanted no part of what that life offered. But Tonia also knew that this "normal" life left Mike feeling like something was always missing. That feeling was more apparent for Mike after 9/11. All the job changes, the different hobbies, even his efforts to become a police officer still left Mike feeling empty. Despite the April Fool's shock, Tonia knew in her heart Mike's decision to join the Reserves was what he needed. It was this decision that satisfied the void in his life and completed his need to serve.

John Eldredge, in his powerful book *Wild at Heart*, writes specifically about men searching to find their purpose, and their longing to satisfy the void and recover their masculine heart. Eldredge wrote "God designed men to be dangerous." Whether or not you believe in God isn't the point. Every boy from the moment he can walk seeks danger or trouble, and all sticks become a sword or gun to aid in the conquest. This feeling stays with men through-out adulthood. Eldredge goes on to say, "Simply look at the dreams and desires written in every boy's heart: to be a hero, to be a warrior, to live a life of adventure and risk." Mike was only answering the calling on his heart, as many others before him have done. And the military offers the option for many men and women to answer that calling.

Brotherhood

That sense of belonging to something great doesn't necessarily fade over time either. "There is a tremendous brotherhood [in the military]." Lt. Cmdr Miller, whom I met through a mutual friend, echoed a close to universal feeling of many service members. He was career military, retired from the service after 23 years and at the age of 50 was considering coming out of retirement to rejoin in the "brotherhood." He had made a successful career for himself in civilian life, but he missed that sense of belonging to something great.

For Lt. Cmdr Miller, it was about the relationships. Sure, he had made professional relationships in the corporate world, but none quite like the ones he made while in the service. Relationships are defined and refined through the good times but even more so through the rough times. In the military you learn to work out conflicts and to relate to others who are experiencing similar situations. You quickly become solution oriented simply because you can't divorce yourself from the situation. As a result, strong bonds are often formed. You face the conflict and work through it together.

Throughout both his active duty and reserve service there were times Lt. Cmdr Miller participated in hostile conflicts. Because each day held unknowns, there was comfort in knowing he could count on the members of his unit.

Maneuvering through dangerous conflict often brings the members of a unit closer because their lives depend on it. As a result, there is often a lifelong brotherhood formed that few outsiders can understand.

Like Miller, most young men and women want and need to belong to something. Look at the impact and influence YouTube, Facebook, MySpace and the many other social networking companies have on today's youth; more importantly, look at the size of these networks! If you don't belong to a network – today's term for brotherhood – you aren't "hip" and you certainly aren't in the "know." This community has its own language, its own acronyms, and its own protocol. Sound familiar? However, what these networks lack is direction and discipline. To its advantage the military offers a definite direction and discipline.

After the high school brotherhood, some of us join our friends at the local mill – and form another brotherhood; others of us run off to college or get a job and with that, we form another brotherhood...and then there are some who join the service. You get the picture. We adapt to our situation, work to develop some sort of internal network of people we can trust so that we can have others around us who share in and understand our experiences.

Corporations attempt to create this same environment but because their focus is more on the bottom line they often fail to create a lasting bond with employees. In order to get ahead often means someone has to lose; so your cubicle friend is your lunch buddy, but after lunch you are working aggressively to out position him or her.

This is where the military has an advantage. In the military there is a sense of order and respect where all parties are working toward a common cause.

I occasionally take my daughter to her swim lessons and on one such occasion I met a young lady, Summer, whose son had attended the earlier lesson. Summer is an amazing woman with three kids under the age of six. Talk about someone who can manage chaos…she made it look easy. Her husband was prior active duty Air Force and now flew cargo planes in the Air Force Reserves. She raved about the brotherhood of active duty life. What she said next took me by total surprise. Despite the war and world conflicts, she was encouraging her husband to return to active duty because she loved that feeling of belonging and everyone having a common cause. Summer found the 'keeping up with the Jones' mentality' of suburban civilian life, frustrating. She and her civilian neighbors often weren't able to relate because everyone was "doing their own thing."

I pressed her a bit for a clearer explanation and she simply said that when she and her husband lived on base it seemed they not only had more time for the kids, but that she had more in common with her neighbors. All the neighbors on base lived in similar housing so there was no impressing your neighbor with your home and she could relate to her neighbors because they were experiencing similar situations. There was camaraderie and a sense of belonging that was missing in their civilian life. She missed the brotherhood.

It was quite evident that even after leaving the military, that sense of belonging to something great had a positive, lasting impression on Mike and Lt. Cmdr Miller as well as Summer and her husband. The chances of finding this sense of purpose or feeling of belonging in suburban corporate America is quite slim, especially in today's market.

Joining or Re-enlisting in the Service

Most of you reading this book are already a member of one of the service branches – even so, it is vital you take the time to remember "why" you considered joining the service in the first place. If you are considering joining, your "why" must be crystal clear – especially today. This reflective exercise will create a stronger foundation for success in your military career and your marriage. It is imperative to discuss and communicate the "why" behind your decision with your spouse.

Recognize that marriages, like missions, are severely compromised when communication breaks down, as was evident by Tonia's initial response. When you communicate what you want to do with your life to your spouse, whether it includes the military or civilian life, you are building trust and intimacy in the relationship. To avoid doing this puts you at a tremendous risk for divided expectations.

New Horizons

So how do you confidently walk through the decision making process so you know what to communicate? Get educated. There are a number of good resources available that will aid you in your research. Questions like, How can you be certain your decisions are anchored in reason and not emotion? If you are considering joining the military for the first time, consider the following:

There is a great website www.military.com that highlights all the services – Army, Navy, Air Force, Marines, Coast Guard, Air National Guard, Army National Guard, Special Operations, ROTC, etc. It is designed to specifically walk the newest person through questions and explanations of each branch. It also has a job interest survey and ASVAB practice tests. If you don't know what the ASVAB is, best to check out the site. The site also provides a ten step process for joining the military. The following is a quick overview of the site:

Step 1   *Learn about the military*: become familiar with the history and mission of the branch that interests you most and understand where they deploy around the world.

Step 2   *Decide if you are ready*: for anything in life to be successful, there is prep work. Do your homework; know what it takes to be eligible for the branch of service you are interested in. Know what benefits are made available and determine if your personal goals matches the branch's mission statement.

Step 3   *Choose the right path*: this is a life decision. Is this only a chapter in your life, with the intent of catapulting your civilian career, or is your life career going to be serving the country? Know your point of entry; are you going to join as an enlisted member or as an officer? Are you considering active duty or reserve/guard service? What job do you want to perform?

Step 4   *Meet the recruiter*: it is important that you have completed steps 1 thru 3 before this step. If you don't have a clear understanding of what you want, you will be directed to where *they* need you. No different than life really. If you don't go after what you want in life, you'll get what life gives you…the leftovers.

Step 5   *Ace the ASVAB*: this stands for Armed Services Vocational Aptitude Battery and covers Arithmetic Reasoning, Word Knowledge, Paragraph Comprehension and Mathematics Knowledge. Take the practice exams. The score determines whether you are qualified to join the military; how well you score determines how qualified you are for certain military occupations.

Step 6   *Get the best job*: this is your future. You have the opportunity to select what career path you want to pursue. Put some thought into this. The site has a tremendous tool called Interest Matcher that allows you to select the box next to your interest and then it will match your interests to military occupations.

Step 7   *Complete the process*: before you join, you'll be sent to Military Entrance Processing Station

(MEPS); it is here that the military will determine if you are healthy and smart enough to be a member of the military. Know the requirements.

Step 8   *Raise your right hand*: know what it means to be sworn in; this section will prepare you for boot camp, give you a heads-up on rank structure, oaths and general orders you'll want to know before making your way to boot camp.

Step 9   *Get ready for boot camp*: boot camp for most is a wake up call. Mom is not there to take care of you. Boot camp is designed to retrain you mentally and prepare you for one of the most rewarding chapters in your life. Be prepared. Know what to bring; read up on some of the boot camp tips and compare the different training programs from each branch.

Step 10 *You're in! Make the most of it*: once you survive boot camp you become part of the brotherhood. This is where your journey really begins. Discover tips on how to handle your military career and learn from other famous veterans on how they maneuvered through their careers. You can design your future and you will have support.

Joining the service can be and should be one of the most rewarding decisions you make in your life. You'll ensure this is the case by working through these ten steps. Visit the site for more detailed explanations of each step.

If at any point through these steps you hesitate or have questions, find the answers before making this important decision.

Factors to Consider When Enlisting

Regardless of whether you are single or married, the decision to join requires that you take certain factors into consideration. These factors are going to vary depending on your situation, but there are certain key elements that are universal to each recruit and must be considered:

1. *You will likely see combat if you join today's military.* Today's military branches are placed in a combat deployment cycle. Know what that cycle is for your branch. Are you prepared for and willing to face the effects of multiple combat deployments?

2. *Your family will be influenced and affected by your decision to join.* Be prepared to explain your decision and know that your decision will be questioned out of love and fear.

3. *Your decision and what you experience will remain with you for the rest of your life.* This really applies to any major decision you make in your life – and it especially applies to your decision to enlist or re-enlist. Be aware that there is a chance you will die honorably in combat. There is a better chance that you won't die but that you could be severely injured. Those who serve in combat return with few life threatening issues; but be prepared to live with your experiences for the rest of your life. You will also develop some lifelong friend-

ships and great memories that will put a smile on your face during some of the oddest moments

The above list is short and only a starting point. Add to this list and have everyone in your inner circle contribute to the list. You can move confidently forward in your decision when you and others have put some educated thought into the decision and have thoroughly discussed your list.

Walking Through the Decision to Re-enlist

So what if you are considering re-enlistment? Patriotism and emotion will only carry the decision to re-enlist so far. Chances are you have had boots on ground in one of several combat zones so you are most likely aware of the effects your military service has had on both you and family members. You understand that to be born in this country is a blessing and to join the greatest military force in the world is an honor. The first you had no control over, but the decision to re-enlist needs to be anchored in solid reasoning. You must be able to answer the question "Why do you want to re-enlist?" with something a bit deeper than "I want to fight for my country" or "the bonus is enticing."

In his book *Visioneering*, Andy Stanley fleshes out the reasoning behind decisions. He poses the question "Why should I attempt this?" Instead of asking "Why should I attempt this?" ask yourself "Why should I re-enlist?" Stanley expands on the question "Why should I attempt this?" by asking "why" after each of his answers. By continually asking "why" the dialogue is forced to move from the realm of circumstance to one focused on values. Is your decision to re-enlist values based?

Your choices and the decisions you make confirm or compromise your values, whether you realize it or not. So ask yourself "why" and be sure the answers match up with your values.

Bestselling author John Maxwell provides a short cut on getting to the core of your decision and ensuring it is values based:

1. *Weigh out the options in front of you.*
2. *Ask if those choices force you to compromise personal values.*
3. *Seek wise counsel.*
4. *Count the cost.*
5. *Decide based on principles.*
6. *Act on your decision swiftly and firmly.*

Go to "Ben"

Another way to flesh out the core of your decision is to utilize the Ben Franklin Pros and Cons List. When I was growing up my dad would sit me down and we'd go through the Ben Franklin process. I'd get out my sheet of white paper, draw a line down the center, write Pros on one side of the line and Cons on the other. And then my dad would loft relevant questions my direction and I'd have to decide if my answer was a pro or a con. I grew to absolutely hate the Ben Franklin exercise. I had absolutely no patience for the process and would rather make a decision quickly, right or wrong, and deal with the results of that decision later. Well, that quick-draw strategy can work to decide where to get your latte or where to get your oil changed, but that's about it. As much as I hated the process then, most of my decisions today are still made using the pros and cons list. Do this and you'll see how complicated decisions become quite simple. My guess is you'll have a sense of peace about you when the exercise is completed.

Both Maxwell and Franklin's processes are effective – and depending on your personality, both can be irritating and painful. But remember, this is a major life decision and what little irritation or pain this process may cause you now will likely save you major irritation and pain in the future. A life decision is just that – a life decision. Your decision to join or re-enlist is a life decision. You will live with it for the rest of your life, so be sure you do your due diligence and then act on it. And when you do decide, you will do so with confidence.

Bringing It Home

★ ★ ★

Strategy #1 for strengthening your marriage

We join for a number of reasons – to start a new life, a deeper calling to serve a cause greater than ourselves, for camaraderie, etc. Determine your life vision as a couple. Map out your marriage mission plan and determine how the military plays a role in that plan.

Questions to consider:

1. What are your reasons for serving or considering serving this country?

   _____

   _____

   _____

   _____

   _____

2. What do you wish to give and get from your service?

   _____

   _____

   _____

   _____

3. What concerns does your spouse have regarding your decision?

_____

_____

_____

_____

4. What sources have you sought out to aid in your decision?

_____

_____

_____

_____

5. What makes your decision values based?

_____

_____

_____

_____

Final Thought: *There is a price to your need and commitment to make a difference. It could be your life; it could be the time away from your spouse and children. Your commitment to make a difference will change your life forever.*

CHAPTER 2

Preparing Your Marriage for Deployment

"No amount of mental preparedness will slow the tears – expect tears."

If you don't tell us when you are going to go, we are going to tell you. When Cheryl's husband Peter, the supply officer for a unit in Oregon, shared the news with her that he needed to volunteer or "be volunteered" for a tour in Afghanistan, her mind began reeling. They had met twenty some years ago while he attended the University of Idaho and ROTC was his way of following in his family's footsteps…and to pay for college. Five children later, she now worried and struggled with constantly changing deployment dates and the unknown possibilities that come with being a war bride. *Is he really going to go or is he not going to go? Can this really be happening? What about the kids?* Cheryl held on to the belief that the events of the war would change. Needless to say, there were a lot of talks and a lot of tears.

Every waking minute you are thinking about the day they leave. I had to keep busy…three to four days before he left Peter was gone morning to night for prep. But the last month before he left, he took a lot of time off work. He kidnapped the kids from school and we went on picnics – he did an individual "date night" with each one of our kids. Peter sat down and wrote a letter to each of the family members. The week before deployment I cried the whole week.

Cheryl readily admitted that no amount of mental preparation erased the emotions she faced before deployment. Where do you even start in preparing yourself, let alone your marriage, for the reality of how deployment will affect your relationship with your spouse, your children and your family? Grief, sadness and hope will compete on a daily basis. There are things you can do to prepare your marriage so that you can successfully survive deployment. Peter and Cheryl made a conscience effort to succeed.

First Steps

One of the first steps Peter took in preparing his marriage for deployment was to organize and prepare a binder with all the information in it he thought Cheryl would need. Take this a step further by asking your spouse what information he or she needs. The binder included everything from electricians and plumbers to life insurance policies, bank PIN numbers, and social security numbers. In most cases, you'll be required by your unit to have all your legal information prepared and on file before deployment. Have this information in the binder as well. By preparing a binder with information he thought would be useful to his wife, Peter removed some of the stress and anxiety Cheryl had regarding his deployment. Granted, it didn't stop all the emotions and there was still plenty of anxiety, but it helped.

One of the other techniques Cheryl and Peter implemented was to set a date to discuss EVERTHING that needed to be talked about and talked through. The alternative, the "pummeling" technique, according to Cheryl was not effective. This is when you assault your spouse with questions, he or she comes back with answers, potential scenarios, etc all at random times and odd moments. Cheryl shared that

> *pummeling each other with all this information caused major frustration for both of us, so we set a date, put the kids away and agreed to talk about everything that needed to be talked about on an agreed upon night; anything that came up prior to the date we jotted down and saved for that date.*

How much EVERYTHING can there truly be to discuss? If you've only been married for a few months, the answer to this question is pretty obvious. But if you've been married for any serious length of time, sharing everything from crazy kid moments to intimate marriage moments you'd think there wouldn't be much to discuss – until you realize the magnitude and meaning of deployment. And then, like Cheryl, you realize how much you really haven't discussed with your spouse.

Ask yourself these simple questions:

If my spouse were to leave for twelve to fifteen months, starting tomorrow:

1. Would I know where everything is?
2. What bills need to be paid?
3. Where all the important paperwork is filed?

If you prepare the binder, some of these questions should already be answered, but there are a ton more questions you should ask.

Revealing EVERYTHING

As Keri and I were driving back home after the interview with Cheryl, we began to talk about just how much we hadn't discussed in our own marriage. Like most couples, we took each other for granted, not really paying attention to the details we each knew that makes our day-to-day lives and our marriage work. In some ways, we were independent managers of the same marriage, tripping over each other in some areas and totally ignorant of what the other was doing in other areas. We realized we were managing our business better than our marriage. So we decided to implement a weekly meeting where we'd discuss *everything*.

Setting a date and sticking to it is not easy; as a matter of fact, it is much easier to employ the ineffective pummeling technique. Set a meeting to discuss *everything* in order to better prepare your marriage for deployment.

Here are a couple of suggestions to get the "revealing everything" process started:

Lightning Round: this technique is used throughout the financial and business world. The team leader asks each team member what one issue – the most pressing issue – he or she would like to bring to the table for discussion. The topics that are brought to the table are the only topics that are addressed in that particular meeting. The reasoning behind this is so the team leader can provide direction in areas his or her team deem critical. This keeps the team focused, engaged and working together toward a common solution – solutions the team deem important.

You and your spouse are the team. Fortunately, there are only two of you! Sit down with each other and a sheet of paper to list the most pressing issues you need answers. Alternate back and forth, asking each other anything. This is not the time to answer the questions, just to list them. Get all the issues on paper before you address them. If you think there are a lot of questions to resolve, set two different dates; one date you allow your spouse to bring up his or her questions and you address them and then the following date you bring up your questions and get them addressed. It's a good idea to set another meeting date at least a week prior to deployment as well. On this day first review all the questions and answers, then address any additional issues that might arise during the discussions.

Check List: another approach is to keep a pocket notebook with you at all times. As you go about your day, jot down questions you have for your spouse, or topics you need to discuss with your spouse prior to deployment. This technique is rather effective simply because your questions or topics are often triggered by the situations or events you experience throughout the day, whereas the Lightning

Round relies on your memory to conjure all questions and topics at once.

Regardless of what technique you use, agree as a couple that everything is fair game. The only rules are that the conversation can't be one-sided and that there is equal consideration for all concerns. There should be no questions left unanswered or topics not discussed when you or your loved one deploys. The key is to have NO REGRETS.

Questions to Ask

Most people spend more time preparing for a weekend away or a weeklong vacation than they spend thinking about the future. Think about your last getaway as a couple. Chances are, you had a checklist, checked it several times, whether it was a suitcase or the car, you likely checked, packed and repacked each several times…and if you have kids, I am CERTAIN there were multiple checks! There are probably other times when you jump in the car and go but if the trip stretches beyond two days, checklists are employed, multiple conversations are had (some borderline nagging) and there seems to be an endless stream of questions. Preparing for deployment should be no different. As a matter of fact, this event should be treated as the most important checklist and conversation you've had since you decided to marry. And the questions you ask need to delve deep.

As Cheryl shared, just the thought of Peter deploying was overwhelming and so was what questions to ask. How to prepare for deployment can often get jumbled in countless competing emotions, so to ensure you cover most topics faced in a marriage, separate your questions into categories: My Home, My Health, Myself. If you have children, consider how you want to involve them and get their questions answered.

My Home

Any questions you have regarding your home, including finances, needs to be placed in this category:

1. When is the mortgage due?

2. When are property taxes due?

3. What company insures the home? When is insurance due? How is it paid – auto-withdrawal or do you need to write a check? (TIP: according to one chaplain, the more bills you can place on auto-pay the better – this will relieve some of the anxiety of when to pay what.)

4. What utilities need to be paid? When? What types of utilities services do you have? Where are the invoices filed?

5. Where do you get the money to pay the bills? When do you get paid?

6. If general repairs need to be made, who should be called? Plumbing? Electrical?

7. Where is the water shut-off valve located? Where is the electrical panel located?

8. What upkeep is necessary on a monthly or quarterly basis?

9. Is there ever a need to sell the house and if so, at what point do you need to sell the house?

This list is just a starting point and you'll likely come up with more questions as you and your spouse share moments in your home.

My Health

This can be a really tough topic because in some ways you are dealing with what-ifs. Health is a broad topic that covers everything from, *"What do I do if my spouse is no longer able to decide or communicate his or her preferences?"* to *"How do I decide between life and death?"* These are not easy questions. But think of this as life preparation. Most couples fail to plan this part of their life because it truly is difficult discussing worst-case scenarios. However, having this discussion and considering a course of action will provide tremendous security and relief for both you and your spouse.

Prior to deployment, the military will have you prepare a Last Will and Testament. The process is time consuming; however, knowing in advance what to do in a given scenario, no matter how grim or tragic, is always better than a forced decision during such a situation. It is best you have an idea of how you want your estate to be carried out prior to the preparation of this document.

Your Last Will and Testament will fall within the directives mandated by your state of residence so if you have one already prepared, check with your command legal department to confirm that your Will is sufficient. There are complicated Wills, depending on your assets, and then there are simple Wills. Be sure to consult with your legal counsel regarding what type of Will best fits your family. In our case, we have a Living Trust in addition to our Will. At a minimum, your Will should address the following:

Article One: My Family – this section lists my spouse and my children.

Article Two: Guardians of My Children – this section essentially says that if your spouse does not survive you, you appoint the following individual or couple to care for your children.

Article Three: Distribution of My Property – this is where you decide who gets what.

Article Four: Powers of My Personal Representative – you will be asked to name a personal representative to administer your estate; in this section you direct what powers and authorities your representative will have.

Article Five: Payment of Expenses and Taxes and Tax Elections – the saying, "the only sure thing in this world is death and taxes" applies here. Not to make light of a grim event, but when one dies, there is a death tax and this section covers such an event.

Article Six: Appointment of My Personal Representative – in most cases you will appoint your spouse as your personal representative. If you and your spouse are both serving in the military, you may want to consider appointing someone who is not serving.

Each page of this document will be initialed and witnessed. The final page will be an Affidavit of Attesting Witnesses. You will either be asked to bring two witnesses with you or the military will provide the witnesses. The document will then be notarized. If you stop here, then at least you've provided a basic road map that maneuvers through potential scenarios.

What Is a Health Care Directive?

What is a Health Care Directive and why should you consider having one? In the simplest of terms, this document addresses your right as an adult to control your own medical care by consenting to or refusing medical treatment. It also provides instructions to your agent on how to carry out your health care wishes.

Essentially, a Health Care Directive is a tool which allows you to:

- Appoint another person (called an agent) to make health care decisions for you if you become unable to communicate decisions, or for that matter, are unable to make decisions for yourself.

- Leave written instructions so that others can make decisions based on your wishes and preferences, or

- Do both – appoint a health care agent and leave detailed instructions.

This is a really tough topic. There are certain discussions we as couples don't want to undertake because we don't want to think about them. Deployment forces the issue. It is important that you and your spouse communicate your wishes and expectations on prolonging life artificially, and that you both understand and agree what defines a terminal condition or a permanent unconscious condition. The medical issues surrounding PTSD will likely fall in this category as well. Discuss how you will help each other through this issue should it impact your marriage.

Myself

We all love talking about ourselves – and this is where you get to do exactly that. Unfortunately, the topics aren't likely to be the same ones you discussed when you were dating. Cheryl recalled talking a lot with Peter about the deployment issue and because they did so, there was some comfort, if only slight. However, she also said that every time the topic of deployment came up, she cried.

Writing questions down and categorizing them into topics will certainly help break through some discomfort and help organize your thoughts. It may seem funny at first to write down topics or questions you would normally talk about off the cuff. But remember, these categories are here to reduce the pummeling feeling and to ensure everything is covered. If there was ever a time to manage your relationship and have a battle plan in place, it is now.

As easy as talking about yourself sounds, this is where you are likely going to encounter one of your first major hurdles. For Peter and Cheryl, walls had already been erected because they didn't start to truly prepare themselves or their marriage for deployment until they had the orders in hand. It was easy to deal with the details... the questions regarding the home and what needed to get done before leaving; but relating on an emotional level, that was another story. Cheryl found herself staying busy and avoiding emotional topics just so she wouldn't think about the looming departure date. And the same went for Peter. In addition, as mentioned earlier Peter was preparing for the unit's deployment from sun up to sundown three days prior to his deployment so for self-preservation he had already started the process of disengaging from his family. Cheryl shared that she never really was "prepped," so she didn't know what to expect and felt like she didn't handle her thoughts and emotions well. It was easier to not think about what was about to happen than to bring up any emotional topics. During this time it almost seems it is better to leave things unsaid than to address them. No matter how difficult, share your thoughts, share your feelings, and establish ground rules for communication.

One of the most important steps a couple can take prior to deployment is to develop a communication game plan. As a couple accustomed to living together, you are used to sharing both the good and the bad of your day with your spouse when you get home. Most couples tend to follow the same pattern when first deployed and this can lead to serious tension in the relationship.

Here are a few guidelines to follow:

1. There is nothing wrong with talking about how you feel. Before you or your spouse deploys, determine how you will let each other know how much you miss and love each other. Ask each other what is appropriate to share across the miles.

2. This point may seem to be in direct conflict with the above point, but it really isn't: **determine what you are NOT going to talk about.** Make sure your conversations don't become dumping grounds. One soldier shared that his wife, during one of their phone conversations, was complaining about how the toilet kept backing up; though a huge issue to her, this issue seemed so tedious to him. First off, in his mind, he felt she should be thankful she had a running toilet and two, because he couldn't be there to solve the problem, just knowing about it made him feel frustrated and helpless.

3. Write down the qualities you most appreciate about your spouse and then share your list. This list will reaffirm to your spouse why you cherish your relationship and it will also provide a connection and reminder of what's important when you are deployed.

Soldiers openly admitted that because of the missions they were involved in, it was easier to disconnect and not have emotional ties to home. In their minds, this was what kept them focused on their mission and kept them alive in the field. All they truly wanted to know was that they had the love and support of their family when they spoke to them across the miles. You will need to determine, as a couple, how best to communicate this message…whether it is verbally or in writing.

Creating Your Support Network

Cheryl admitted that it was approximately twelve months into Peter's deployment before she heard from the military support network. Typically for Reservists and Guard the Family Readiness Group is manned by volunteers, so understand that, depending on your location, you may not have someone calling you on a monthly basis. Also be aware you may not have a close network of other spouses who are about to go through what you will experience. For this reason, it is important to establish your support network in advance.

1. Find those friends and family members who are willing to be a supportive ear for your spouse who is manning the home front.

2. If you have children, ask relatives to occasionally provide your spouse with relief or to help out around the house.

3. Be prepared to keep a list detailing what someone can do to help. Depending on how well you establish your support network, your friends and family will ask if there is anything they can do to help. Welcome the help and let them know what they can do to help.

It may be difficult finding other civilian spouses who will relate to what you go through. However, it is unlikely you will be the only military spouse or couple in your community who will experience separation due to deployment. Check with your local church, the VET center, even the Family Readiness Group to determine what other couples in your community are in a similar situation. Your family is going to be very supportive; however, you will likely relate better and find strength in spending time and sharing your thoughts with someone who is experiencing, or who is about to experience your same scenario.

If you are about to deploy, one of the best foundations you can leave your spouse is the preparation of how the future may look and what to expect to endure. Your marriage is a partnership and now half of the partnership is going on an "extended business trip" that is dangerous. To inform your partner of what life may look like with half the partnership operating at a distance will provide a tremendous sense of peace and security, as well as direction and hope. When you are done, listen to your spouse's perspective on what the future holds back at home. A successful marriage is one that is built not on dominance but on mutual respect. Share your side and then make the time to listen.

BRINGING IT HOME

✯ ✯ ✯

Strategy #2 for strengthening your marriage:

Prepare each other for deployment and mentally walk your spouse into what *you* believe the future holds for your marriage and your family.

Questions to consider:

1. Treat your separation as part of the mission. What have you done to prepare each other and your family for deployment? Is your plan written down?

   _____

   _____

   _____

   _____

   _____

2. Have you asked all the questions you need to ask each other? Be sure there are NO REGRETS.

   _____

   _____

   _____

   _____

3. Have you developed a game plan for staying connected? The deployment cycles are longer and more frequent, and this can certainly put a great deal of strain on your relationship. What tools have you identified to stay connected? (Video, Internet, IM, phone, letters, etc.)

_____

_____

_____

_____

4. What are your off limit subject matters when you are communicating during deployment?

_____

_____

_____

_____

5. What family members have been notified of the upcoming deployment? Have they been notified on how best to help during this time?

_____

_____

_____

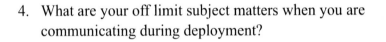

6. What organizations or clubs in your community offer assistance or provide support for families that experience deployment separation?

_____

_____

_____

_____

Final Thought: *Prepared marriages stand ready to meet the future. By being prepared, you will move forward with confidence and won't easily be surprised.*

CHAPTER 3

Emotional Turmoil: The First Few Weeks

"It's a depression"

The minute Peter left, Cheryl got sick. *I'm sick, my house is torn apart, and I can't even lie down in my bed.* Her house was under construction, new windows were being put in and within the week she had to rush her youngest son to the ER because he got a Lego stuck up his nose. *The first week was terrible, I just wanted to sit down and cry.*

Jody's first week with Army Reserve husband Brian deployed was following a similar path. Brian's tour was slotted for only a four month rotation; though a blessing compared to what many soldiers must serve, it didn't make the situation any easier.

I saw a lot of people the first week and they'd say, "Jody, you just don't look the same" and I'd think to myself, "what do you want me to look like?" Friends, not sure what to say, would attempt to comfort her by letting her know that she "just looked sad." Jody assured them that she was.

As Jody shared, *you get through it*. For Jody and Cheryl, there was no strong network of civilian wives turned military in their community. Distance from other spouses in the unit prevented any family support get-togethers or outings and there was very little "informational stuff." These two women happened to find each other because they attended the same church.

For spouses of regular active duty members, the lifestyle active duty offers includes a built-in support team. There is a brotherhood and a network that comes with the career choice. What Jody, Cheryl and others found, coming from reserve to active lifestyle, was that they needed to develop their own support network.

If you are the spouse who is staying behind – or being left behind, as one spouse so aptly put it – you might feel there is nothing you can do to make the first few weeks bearable. But be assured, there are a few things you can do to help yourself; and there are a few things you can do to safe guard yourself from falling into a funk.

Making the First Week Bearable

My buddy. This was Jody's answer when asked what helped her get through the first week. When asked if there was a strong network of military wives to plug into or if the military facilitated any introductions, she just laughed and said, "No." If you are coming from the Reserves or Guard, be prepared to plan your course of action. Decide in advance WHAT you need to do and how you will keep your thoughts on the positive when there is limited support. Then be prepared to execute.

In business, the three magic words used to be location, location, location. In your marriage, especially a marriage that is about to experience a separation due to deployment, the magic words are plan, plan, plan. Advance planning will help you make the first few weeks bearable. Making a connection with someone through your church, the PTA or some other organization that has experienced or is experiencing a similar situation will provide some comfort. It may seem awkward to seek out a relationship at first, as both Jody and Cheryl admitted. They initially shied away from meeting each other at church for that very reason. They were aware of each other and knew that they shared a similar circumstance but it wasn't until they felt they had nowhere else to go did they turn to each other.

It's perfectly normal to think you can handle your situation; after all, why would this be any different from an extended business trip? Shouldn't you just be able to buck up and keep going without any support? Don't count on it.

Here are a few suggestions to ease the pain and slow the tears:

1. Establish your support network before deployment. Jody and Cheryl finally took the steps to meet and get acquainted. When Brian deployed, Jody could turn to Cheryl for support and vice versa. Cheryl understood Jody's pain and could relate and provide comfort.

2. Every military organization has a family support program. Stay in touch with your command's family support office. They will be able to direct you to resources and provide answers. Make them work and do not take no for an answer when you have a need.

3. Prepare your network. Although you won't necessarily be able to predict what your exact emotions will be those first few weeks, chances are, you'll have a good idea of how you "may" be. Let your friends and family know what to expect and how they can best help you through this time. Preparing your family and friends is just as important as preparing yourself.

Preparing Your Family and Friends for the First Few Weeks

You have enough to think about and you certainly don't want to think about having to prepare your friends and family for this looming deployment. The thought of preparing just yourself and your children brings you to tears. Shouldn't your friends and family be looking for ways to comfort you and prepare you, whether you are the soldier or the spouse? Yes and no. Without question, your true friends will ask what they can do to help, but out of sheer ignorance they'll need your help to help you. You'll need to manage your comfort and not rely on someone else to manage it for you.

Your friends and family will likely need very little coaching or reminding of your needs or situation when you or your spouse first deploys. It's the weeks and months after the first couple of weeks where they may need help. You must prepare them for the longevity of the deployment. *At first, everyone clamored around, and then they (meaning her friends and family) go away.* Jody continued, *they forget. I can't blame people – life goes on – and it doesn't affect anybody until it happens to them. People think, 'I don't want to bother her'...it is not a bother! Put it on the calendar to stay in touch.*

Jody's suggestions, listed below, will benefit you and your family. They will also help prepare your network on ways they can stay connected to you:

1. Remind your network, and TELL your network, how they can stay connected beyond the first two weeks. Let them know the best way to reach you: email, phone, IM, letter, etc.

2. Have someone offer to take the kids to school if you have children. This will help keep an outside influence around your children.

3. Suggest play dates if you have children. Cheryl mentioned that she and Peter had one friend who consistently stayed in touch with her and the children.

4. Tell one of your friends or a family member – one you preferably like – to put on his/her calendar to call you once a week.

5. If someone is a great cook, ask if they are open to making double the amount of food and putting you down as a recipient.

6. Remind your network of both your children's and spouse's birthdays and ask if they will send them cards. This will make a huge impact on your children and you. One spouse mentioned that when she received an anniversary card from a friend, it helped her realize that her friends did care. She later found out that her husband received a card as well and it meant the world to him.

It may seem awkward to make requests, but what you'll find is that most of your network is searching for ideas on how best to support you anyway. So provide them with the ideas.

As my wife Keri and I were sitting around the table with Jody and Cheryl on a follow-up interview, my wife had the insight to ask a simple but very revealing question, "What do you wish friends would do more of" and almost simultaneously Jody and Cheryl said, "CALL." They both wished they had prepared their network of friends and family to call more frequently. You need someone Cheryl chimed in and then she continued, *a lady from church called and I just started bawling; a lady I didn't even really know just calling to tell me about Bible study...and then people started calling again. People didn't want to intrude...I'm sure I've done this to someone else...I wish people would call more.* Prepare your network and let them know what you think you will need. In addition to what you need, be sure to inform them of what you don't need. This will save you from some grief and hard feelings.

What You Don't Need from Your Network

Tonia also admitted that she was a wreck the first few weeks. *I was pretty emotional the whole time but mostly kept it to [myself] when I was driving to and from work. Certain songs got me pretty upset...I just lived day by day.* If you have children, it will be especially tough. You may even have absolute feelings of rage at your spouse, especially when you see how your children react to the deployment. Your family will be a mixed bag of emotions and the last thing you need is for your network to do something stupid. Tonia shared what she didn't need and what didn't help so you can avoid a similar situation.

A lot of our family (aunts, uncles, cousins) were totally against the war and made it well known. They would ask me "what was Mike thinking re-enlisting" or "that was the stupidest thing he has ever done." This part of our family actually did not talk to me or have any part of our lives the whole time of Mike's deployment. Some family must have felt that since they were related they could give us their opinions. One family member actually called to tell me that Mike had his priorities in the wrong place. Another thing that didn't help was people that just didn't listen. Instead of just listening to what I had to say, they would have pretty insensitive comebacks or try to fix my problems. Early on in the deployment I was trying to talk to an immediate family member about how hard it is; the family member strongly urged her opinion on me that I needed to see a doc-

tor and take medication. Instead of just listening, agreeing that "yes, this is hard," and being supportive, this person tried to fix my problem her way. I never talked about what I was going through to this person again. Some people would be uncomfortable and not know what to say so they would just come up with something. One of my co-workers told me, "now I know what you feel like having your spouse in danger." Well, she didn't know what it was like; her husband was making that choice to go [recreational] flying. Yes, my husband made the choice to go into the Army but he didn't make the choice to be shot at, to have bombs explode next to him and to mortared on his base everyday.

Be prepared for innocent ignorance especially from family members. The people you are closest with will struggle to relate to your situation the first few weeks of deployment as well. Deployment causes a tremendous change in the family dynamic as well as the social dynamic. Some will approach this time with tough love, others will avoid the topic all together, giving you the impression that they don't care. Some will try to "expert" you through the situation, having no real experience…and yet none will likely take the time to understand how their words and actions will impact you; unless you prepare them in advance. Prepare them. Here's how:

1. Let your friends and family know that you and your spouse are committed to the mission.

2. Inform your network that while you respect their opinions, you don't want to hear them. Tonia once asked a friend why she had never given her opinion and her friend replied, "That is not my place; I am here for you."

Making the First Few Weeks Bearable for Your Children

If you have children, you will need to prepare them – as best you can – on what to expect so that the first few weeks aren't such a huge shock to them as well. Peter wrote each child a letter. Jody had each of her children write their dad Brian a letter. Tonia and Mike told their eldest, who was almost four, that *daddy needed to go to Iraq to help the good people and put the bad people in jail.* However you decide to approach the issue of deployment, be sure you involve your children at an appropriate level and prepare them for the change in your family. In the resource section of this book you will find key websites and books that specifically address the issue of children and deployment.

Regardless of how well you prepare, expect something to go wrong. Peter left on a Tuesday and 10PM Friday night, Cheryl was calling her mother-in-law to stay with the other kids so she could take her son who had lodged a Lego in his nose to the ER. In Jody's case, not even twenty four hours after Brian left, her youngest son had his front teeth knocked out in a wrestling match with his oldest brother.

It is important to recognize that with one spouse gone, the little things are more noticeable and the little events become HUGE; not only to you, but also to your children.

Just know something is going to go wrong...no matter how well you plan, said Cheryl. Originally my motto was "Bring it on" but by the third week I couldn't take it anymore. The fan didn't work; something else was going wrong, the dryer started squeaking...I'm done. And the kids were a basket case. Nobody could replace dad. We did have one man from church write Peter asking if it was okay if he could wrestle with the boys take them on hikes or play basketball...and the children's pastor took the boys to play laser tag. I also had the kids in counseling; a good friend is a counselor so I took advantage of the offer. The military suggested the same, but the paperwork was intimidating.

Brandon, Jody's oldest son, took it the hardest when Brian was gone. It was four months before he understood that he could get on without dad; that dad was still there and that he'd be back.

We had to keep really busy; Brian deployed around Christmas so I had to keep the kids out and involved in lots of activities. There will be moments when you are at your wit's end...you're wanting to leave them in the car and walk away; that's when you call in a family member or friend...preferably sooner!

Expect in the first few weeks that emotions will be at an all-time high. Your children will feed off your emotions. Their first few weeks will be just as emotional for them as they are for you, and depending on the age of your children, they won't be able to explain why.

Here are few things you can do to make their lives a bit more bearable:

1. Sit down as a couple prior to deployment and talk with your children about how the family is going to change.

2. Let your child or children know how they can help out at home while mom or dad is deployed.

3. Plan activities.

4. Breathe life into your children by letting them know that your family is part of an important mission.

And while you prepare your children, just know that the first few weeks for the soldier aren't exactly a cake walk either, as Brian shared.

Brian's Arrival

Hallelujah, I've arrived. I departed my family on the 2nd of December to serve our troops in Kabul, Afghanistan. After 8 days in Ft. Benning, I finally left the mainland. I am now hoping Motrin can decrease the pain from 4 days and six stops worth of military travel on my buttocks. I DO actually believe that I could have swam and hiked here faster, but nonetheless, I've arrived safely and am now breathing a sigh of relief and gratefulness for that. My base is Camp Phoenix and I guess you could say it is as one may expect as far as military post can be in a third world country. I've seen my first flushing toilet in days and there is even a mocha stand. However, outside the base is another story.

Upon arrival to Kabul International Airport (picture a very old Wal-Mart shot up and bombed), we jumped into our body armor and into an array of four wheel drive vehicles that were well-used and abused. I mentioned that they looked as if they had been used as battering rams, two minutes later I found out [why]. They are battering rams and once you are in them you hang on for dear life.

The four lane road to the base was multi-directional and filled with people, animals, children, burning vehicles, and garbage and destruction. It was like a scene from the Apocalypse and absolutely terrifying. Picture a hundred drunks or crack addicts behind the wheel for a rush hour drive with no defined directional flow and you have it. However, a 50 cal mounted on a flying Toyota would get [the locals' attention] and it seemed to work for this trip anyway [providing for safe passage].

In his email Brian described his mission and how the people he would be serving seemed grateful. What he wasn't quite prepared for was the children he would be attending to; the cold conditions were most brutal on them and in his words, *their condition in this cold weather is enough to make you just bawl.*

Life for Brian was drastically different in Afghanistan than it was back at home. No family, no comforts of home (picture concrete buildings with bathroom stall doors that open to holes in the ground), severe weather conditions and an enemy lurking just beyond the wire. Home never seemed so good; but for Brian to cope, he had to think about the mission at hand as his number one priority … and not home.

While Jody and the kids struggled those first few weeks to get their bearings without dad, Brian became immersed in his mission and his new surroundings; and because he did so, he stayed relatively positive.

Safe Guarding Against the Funk

Being a part of the military usually brings a positive response from most…unless our military is involved in a war or some other conflict that is unpopular. And then the opinions fly. Jay Leno, host of The Tonight Show shared his opinion that ruffled feathers but at the same time, offered great insight:

The other day I was reading Newsweek magazine and came across some poll data I found rather hard to believe. It must be true given the source, right?

The Newsweek poll alleges that 67 percent of Americans are unhappy with the direction the country is headed and 69 percent of the country is unhappy with the performance of the president. In essence, two-thirds of the citizenry just ain't happy and want a change.

So being the knuckle dragger I am, I started thinking, "what are we so unhappy about?"

Is it that we have electricity and running water 24 hours a day, 7 days a week? Is our unhappiness the result of having air conditioning in the summer and heating in the winter? Could it be that 95.4 percent of these unhappy folks have a job? Maybe it is the ability to walk into a grocery store at any time and see more food in moments than Darfur has seen in the last year?

Maybe it is the ability to drive from the Pacific Ocean to the Atlantic Ocean without having to present identification papers as we move through each state? Or possibly the hundreds of clean and safe motels we would find along the way that can provide temporary shelter? I guess having thousands of restaurants with varying cuisine from around the world is just not good enough. Or could it be that when we wreck our car, emergency workers show up and provide services to help all and even send a helicopter to take you to the hospital.

Perhaps you are one of the 70 percent of Americans who own a home. You may be upset with knowing that in the unfortunate case of a fire, a group of trained firefighters will appear in moments and use top notch equipment to extinguish the flames, thus saving you, your family and your belongings. Or if, while at home watching one of your many flat screen TVs, a burglar or prowler intrudes, an officer equipped with a gun and a bullet-proof vest will come to defend you and your family against attack or loss.

This is all in the backdrop of a neighborhood free of bombs or militias raping and pillaging the residents. Neighborhoods where 90 percent of the teenagers own cell phones and computers.

How about the complete religious, social and political freedoms we enjoy that are the envy of everyone in the world? Maybe that is what has 67 percent of you folks unhappy.

Fact is we are the largest group of ungrateful, spoiled brats the world has ever seen. No wonder the world loves the U.S. yet has a great disdain for its citizens. They see us for what we are. The most blessed people in the world who do nothing but complain about what we don't have, and what we hate about the country instead of thanking the good Lord we live here.

I know. I know. What about the president who took us into war and has no plan to get us out? The president who has a measly 31 percent approval rating? Is this the same president who guided the nation in the dark days after 9/11? The president that cut tax-es to bring an economy out of recession? Could this be the same guy who has been called every name in the book for succeeding in keeping all the spoiled, ungrateful brats safe from terrorist attacks? The commander-in-chief of an all-volunteer army that is out there defending you and me?

Did you hear how bad the president is on the news or talk shows? Did this news affect you so much, make you so unhappy that you couldn't take a look around and see all the good things and be glad?

Think about it...are you upset at the president be-cause he actually caused you personal pain OR is it because the "media" told you he was failing to kiss your sorry, ungrateful behind every day?

Make no mistake about it. The troops in Iraq and Afghanistan have volunteered to serve, and in many cases may have died for your freedom. There is currently no draft in this country. They didn't have to go. They are able to refuse to go and end up with a "general" discharge, an "other than honorable" discharge, or worst case scenario, a "dishonor-able" discharge after a few days in the brig.

So why then the flat-out discontentment in the minds of 69 percent of Americans? Say what you want but I blame it on the media. "If it bleeds it leads" and they specialize in bad news. Everybody will watch a car crash with blood and guts. How many will watch kids selling lemonade at the corner? The media knows this and the media outlets are for-profit corporations. They offer what sells, and when criticized, try to defend their actions by "justifying" them in one way or another.

Stop buying the negativism you are fed every day by the media. Shut off the TV, burn Newsweek, and use the New York Times for the bottom of your bird cage. Then start being grateful for all we have as a country. There is exponentially more good than bad.

We are among the most blessed people on Earth and should thank God several times a day or at least be thankful and appreciative.

With hurricanes, tornados, fires out of control, mud slides, flooding, severe thunderstorms tearing up the country from one end to the other, and with the threat of bird flu and terrorist attacks, are we sure this is a good time to take God out of the Pledge of Allegiance?

We are so influenced by our surroundings. Whether it is the people you associate with or the books and magazines you read or the shows you watch, your attitude will reflect what you choose to be influenced by.

Jay recommended a few safe guard tips like shutting off the TV and removing the negative from your life. I'm not suggesting you throw out all the magazines, avoid the TV and wrap yourself up in some cocoon to avoid all the negative, but I do encourage you to limit your exposure and take the time to remember WHY you and your family are part of the mission. If you don't know the "why," then sit down with your spouse and figure this out.

The first few weeks are going to be tough, so focusing on your family, on the family vision, and how the military plays into that vision will play a defining role in setting the stage for your survival throughout deployment.

Anything worthwhile has a price to pay. Focus on the prize, not the price. This is definitely vital the first few weeks of deployment and will continue to be critical throughout an extended deployment.

Bringing It Home

★ ★ ★

Strategy #3 for strengthening your marriage:

Take the time to listen to each other. Use the moments you have on the phone to listen to each other and offer encouragement.

Questions to Consider:

1. Who in your network can you share the tough moments with?

   _____

   _____

   _____

   _____

2. Have you prepared your network for the longevity of the deployment?

   _____

   _____

   _____

   _____

3. How are you and your spouse going to help each other through the first few weeks? What is your game plan?

_____

_____

_____

_____

4. How are you and your spouse going to help your children through the first few weeks?

_____

_____

_____

_____

Final Thought: *For most in the Reserve and Guard, long separations were never part of the original marriage plan. Having a vision for how you want your family and your marriage to be will help walk you through this difficult time.*

CHAPTER 4

Living Each Day Apart

"As soon as you can deploy me, deploy me. I didn't join to sit in the States; I joined to go to Iraq or Afghanistan."   *– Mike*

"There were two hard things that stuck out the most when Mike was gone: eating dinner with two toddlers and my husband not sitting across the table where he should be; and no one to hold me and tell me that everything is going to be all right."   *– Tonia*

They were one family living apart who had two different missions in two different worlds. Mike felt compelled to serve; it wasn't about being a hero, this was about giving back to a country that had provided so much. The sooner he could go, the better. *Somebody's got to do it, why should he [someone else] do it and not me?* Life away from his family was part of the mission and part of his job. But for Tonia, life away from Mike was never a part of the plan.

Keeping your worlds together when you are apart takes work. Living each day apart will not be easy. Your experiences will be different, your daily challenges will be different and those life events you are accustomed to sharing together will be fond memories. Mike and Tonia made it work, despite their different worlds. How they did it took effort.

Mike's Mission and World

Mike's military mission was special ops. His personal mission was to stay alive. This "military world" was vastly different from his civilian home life and in order to stay alive and stay sane, he shut down his emotions. *I had to turn myself off over there.*

While deployed, Mike might talk with his daughter once every two weeks. He'd constantly write and draw pictures of his daughter sitting on camels and dinosaurs and send those to her, but to talk with her made it really hard not to become emotional. He kept the link but he limited his exposure. *I had to keep that link because I would see guys that completely shut that link off and what they were turning into over there...they were turning into animals. They were cold; they didn't care. In some of the guys you could see from the time we began, in a few months they saw people get killed, shot, completely blown up, blown up, blown up... pretty soon you could see the coldness in their eyes....*

His mission wasn't pretty. Mosul, where he was stationed, was no place to be walking the streets. Mike usually walked those streets twice a day. *I saw a lot. I went out – they figured it out – over three hundred combat patrols in ten months; that doesn't include the raids I did at night. It's a numbers game. You can only draw the lucky straw so many times. My vehicle was hit seven times with IEDs; three of the times I was in the machine gun position...three of those times; we took several RPGs, people lobbing hand grenades out of buildings at us; but actual roadside bombs that took out parts of the vehicle...seven times.* Mike protected Tonia from these daily events. The last thing he wanted – or needed – was his wife to feel helpless and worried. Her only clue to an event that may have affected Mike was an occasional email that would state "I had a bad day. I love you."

Spiritual Battle

In wars like this, if it was just the enemy combatants, I don't think...that really didn't affect me; it was the kids, the women and the people driving down the street to get groceries...[they] were used in the middle of it...you're driving through a market and you get blown up, you drop rapid ammo to make sure your guys are alright...there's dead kids there; parents are coming out yelling at you about why you did that; I didn't set off the explosion...they blame you...you know...if I was them I'd hate me too. If I wasn't driving down that road, nobody would have blown up that bomb and their kids would still be alive. How could a God make a world so cruel?

Mike left his home strong and confident in his relationship with his God. Each tragic event tested his strength and shook his confidence. So much so that he left his God and had faith only in himself and the guy next to him. Mike liked the idea that Tonia was going to church back home but it wasn't until he returned home that he began to open up and get reacquainted with his God.

Life away changed Mike on the inside and most days were a fight for survival, either emotionally or physically. Tonia's life at home was taking on a new look and new challenges of its own as well. This new separation, both in how they dealt with everyday life and what they believed would later be a gap Mike and Tonia would have to bridge together.

Speaking to the soldier:

1. Mike found a safe place emotionally to hide so he could deal with the daily events. This is normal. But like Mike, find ways to stay connected.

2. Tell your spouse only what they are equipped to handle about your day to day events. Mike kept the details light because he didn't want to add to Tonia's stress. Details will lead to more questions and often an increase in stress and insecurity back home.

3. Stay true to your values and committed to your beliefs. You will have doubt – seek answers.

4. Do your best to encourage your spouse and provide a sense of security and hope. This will make your family's life back home more at ease.

Tonia's Mission and World

Tonia's mission was entirely different than Mike's. When Mike left for Mosul, she figured she basically had three things to do: keep the communication alive between them, keep the kids' lives as normal as possible, and keep herself sane.

*I was hooked on email...if I didn't have an email [from Mike]; I was like...*Tonia's voice trailed off. Mike would email every day, call every three days, but if anyone got killed, the military would shut down all emails. This was the only way the military could control how and when the unfortunate news was communicated to the family. And so if the local news broadcaster stated that a soldier from the Stryker brigade was killed in Mosul, Tonia had no idea if her life with Mike was over.

Life away was an emotional rollercoaster and in many ways awful. Tonia survived but she clearly stated that she would never choose to go through the experience again. It is one thing if, as a husband and wife, you both sign on board for the military lifestyle, it is quite another when you are thrust into the lifestyle because of a decision your spouse made, as Tonia was. Either way, you must decide you are going to make this mission a success.

So Tonia set out to keep herself sane and did her best to keep her children's lives as normal as possible. With her youngest, she would point to pictures of Mike and say "daddy." Mike and Tonia's oldest struggled with life away from daddy. She got more emotional and Tonia found herself having to comfort her daughter's extreme, and completely uncharacteristic, emotional swings. Tonia went from being part of an everyday, normal family unit, to a segregated family unit that was engulfed in emotional upheaval.

I really don't know how I kept sane during this whole process. I had so many "what ifs" happen. There was the time when Mike got pulled off his usual team at the last minute. On patrol that team got hit and two close friends of Mike died. I found myself asking how that happens; Mike goes out with that team 98 percent of the time. I noticed right away that I was on an adrenalin high of "my husband is okay." After about four to five days I would come down from that high and then couldn't stop thinking of the soldiers who were killed and how it just wasn't right. How many times this happened I don't really know. There was the Mosul chow hall bombing which I didn't know if my husband was in or not for a day. Another time I received an email from Mike that he had been injured and would call when he could. It was a long five days before I heard that [he was okay] – a bomb had gone off fifteen feet away from his vehicle and he had been outside of the vehicle operating the turret. The blast had knocked him unconscious and ruptured his ear drum. I shut down a little after that one; I didn't tell anyone about it for two weeks and still only told a few. When Mike knew he was going out for a long mission (usually more

*than three days), he would call home to tell me "I
just wanted to tell you I love you before I go out."
I finally had to tell him he had to stop doing that
because it was like he was calling to talk to me
one more time just in case he didn't make it back.
I definitely noticed a pattern of every time something happened to Mike or should have happened
to Mike…I would have that same high of "he's
okay" and then a crash to "there are so many
other soldiers who are not"…I can honestly say I
am thankful for my kids. I could not have done it
without them; they kept me going.*

Spiritual Rebirth

Tonia readily admitted that Mike was a man of God prior
to his leaving and she, though raised Catholic, had no real
relationship or spiritual foundation whatsoever.

However, life events will sometimes change your beliefs.
While Mike was busy shutting his God out because of
what he saw and what he was doing, Tonia had no place
to turn but to God. But she did it reluctantly. In her mind,
she needed to stay the same so when Mike came home,
she was who he remembered. *I am not going to change
who I am, for when my husband comes back, I need to be
exactly who I am; the house needs to stay the same…I just
sat there thinking 'I am not going to change, I HAVE to
stay the same…and that's when things started to change…
Sometimes there was just so much death, destruction and
'what ifs'; it just got to be too much some times.* She didn't
want to burden her friends, so, she burdened God.

87

Some of you will lean heavily on your faith to get through similar moments; some of you will not. While apart, you will absolutely need to have faith in each other and look for ways to uplift your spouse. You will be greatly challenged by living apart and you both will need encouragement from your spouse.

Speaking to the spouse:

1. At first you will feel lost without your spouse. You will want to know the details of the life being lived by your soldier spouse. Know what you can emotionally handle and communicate that to your spouse.

2. If you have children, focus your efforts on making their lives as "normal" as possible. Deployment affects them as well and if your children are younger, they will not understand the separation. Find ways to keep your children in touch with your spouse and the routine of home life consistent.

3. Be open to change if it fits your family vision. Life at home goes on and change happens daily. Be sure any changes fit with your family vision that you and your spouse established prior to the deployment.

4. Encourage your spouse. Keep your communication positive, yet real. Let your spouse know you've got a handle on the home front in spite of some of the circumstances. Tonia never talked about anything bad or events that would make Mike feel bad that he wasn't at home.

Facing Challenges

For starters, just know that every marriage has its challenges. How you choose to face these challenges as a couple will determine your outcome. If you give yourself an out, then you have failed to commit to moving through the tough times together. Alexander the Great issued his burn the boats strategy when he'd land on enemy shores. This prevented his fellow warriors from retreating, or giving themselves an out when the battle got rough. As Tonia experienced, the battle of being without your spouse will sometimes get to be too much. But she knew that she and Mike would make it because they gave themselves no other choice. Understand though, as angry as you may be or will be because of your experiences with living apart, your spouse is not your enemy. Your spouse is your fellow warrior and the enemy is the challenges that will divide and conquer you as a couple if you are not united. Miles will divide you, but you can be united and brought closer by your commitment to each other.

Overcoming Financial Challenges

In most marriages, money plays a pretty significant role in the relationship and often, if there is a lack of money, it is cause for tremendous strain. Alfie Ramos, Deputy Director for Washington State Department of Veterans Affairs shared that *money is a huge issue that exacerbates other issues*. As a matter of fact, financial frustrations are listed right after poor communication in several studies that track why marriages fail. Knowing this, evaluate your current situation and determine how deployment is going to affect you while you and your spouse are separated. Mike shared that during his trainings it was tough financially...

The hardest part was the training events – the Army does some great things; if you are gone more than 31 days, they pay you extra pay...well, and they'll bring you back in 30 days so they don't have to pay you. And you get housing as a reservist; until you're actually deployed, you get half housing; so if I'm gone a month (normal housing is a $1000/ mo), normally reservists are gone two weeks so I get $500, well if I'm gone a month I still only get the $500...I don't get full housing. You're missing a full month's worth of work, but then I'm only paid partial housing until I'm deployed for longer than six months. Once I was deployed, it was "beneficial" because I got housing, combat pay and all those other things started kicking in...medical.

Once Mike was deployed, financially they were fine. Well, as Tonia said, *as "fine" as one could be in this situation.* Tonia continued to work; Mike sent money; the grandparents were close so they could assist with child care and a friend would occasionally provide some temporary relief. Not all families will have the same experience though.

Unlike Mike and Tonia, where deployment actually provided a pay raise, Brian and Jody had to plan for a pay-cut. Brian was accustomed to working several jobs in order to provide for his four children and Jody occasionally worked a part-time teaching job. Life apart would reduce his multiple sources of income down to one; so Brian made adjustments. He worked longer hours at the ER, pulled more shifts in the clinics and made real estate land deals on the side. Brian knew that living each day apart was going to be stressful enough so he did his best to eliminate any financial frustrations.

TIP: Be sure to discuss and settle financial issues prior to deployment.

Overcoming the Medical Hurdle

Health care is under scrutiny for most Americans; not only those who are serving. However, the government is providing for a new surge in money, some $3.6 billion, to address the many complex issues that soldiers and their families will face throughout deployment and upon return. They are also working to overhaul TRICARE, the military's form of health insurance, so that medical care providers will be more willing to accept TRICARE insurance. In Mike and Tonia's situation, they were fortunate because she worked for a doctor...

What really saved us was her company was the only company that would take TRICARE...only because she worked there. If she hadn't worked at a doctor's office, I don't know what we would have done; nobody wants to take military insurance... because they have the worst reimbursement rates of any insurance. This was the one thing that would have been a major stressor if her company didn't take the insurance. Any government insurance is the worst for the doctor.

So how do you best handle the issue of insurance if you aren't fortunate like Mike and Tonia? If you, as a military spouse, are employed and have medical insurance through a private carrier, be sure you and your children are enrolled. If your only option is TRICARE, contact your State Department of Veterans Affairs or your command's family support office to determine what physicians and clinics are military friendly and will accept TRICARE. As Mike stated, NOT having insurance for his family would have been a major stressor while he was deployed. Be sure you eliminate this stressor.

Finding the "Humor" in Living Apart

You will need to dig deep to make it through these days. Most combat tours will stretch 15 months so birthdays, special events and holidays will be spent without your spouse or your loved ones. Now, if any of you have relatives like the Griswold's or Uncle Eddie, this could be a blessing. For most of you, this will be a difficult time. Tonia found it especially hard because she wanted her family. Jody found it extremely difficult as well and chose to keep busy just so she wouldn't dwell on it. Yet, despite the difficulties and emotions, they dug deep and both found ways to find the humor – and the good – in their situation.

*She enjoyed not having to share the bed, I think…*Mike laughed. And Tonia was quick to admit, with a smile, that after sleeping on his side of the bed for the whole year, it was tough to give it back. Stressful situations are often remedied through humor. If we can laugh at the situation, then we somehow instinctively know that we can make it through the situation. Tonia and Mike both found comfort in bringing humor into their situation.

Most of the time I kept everything very light and good hearted. I remember my husband called home close to Halloween and wanted to know what his little man was going to be. I just couldn't resist and told him a fairy!! Needless to say, he wasn't too happy but now what could he do? What did I do? I decided to take it a step further and dress [her son] up as a fairy – nothing but a diaper, fairy wings and a pink wand. I took a picture and made it into a Christmas card that read "Have a Merry Fairy Christmas!" then mailed it to Mike. Now I was in for it and I knew pay back would be coming. I had told Mike that I deserved compensation for the stress I was under. One day I received a letter with a $10,000 Dinar bill saying I deserve it for all that I do. Well, I took that bill to the bank and it was worth $6.38.

TIP: Mike and Tonia found ways to make each other laugh. They needed to laugh…and so will you.

Finding the "Good" in Living Apart

Brian found the good in his situation and relayed that back to Jody in an effort to make her feel better:

> *It is snowing outside and almost peaceful; the soldiers are scurrying about both excited and downtrodden. They are all away from their loved ones and families as well. There are Xmas decorations all over and the mood is as festive as it can be. I have volunteered to serve chow to the troops and to take a 2 hour guard rotation so that the enlisted can have the day off. I am also on call and have clinic so this will make for a great and fast day for me. It is disappointing that I have to travel across the world to get a white Xmas, but I guess that makes it special in its own right. I can picture the children waking up and being jazzed from their first conscious breath. I do hope that they remember the season and appreciate what they have. Xmas is for kids and we must all remember that, after all it's a child that brought us this great day and we the soldiers that continue to give us the right to celebrate it. I am well and miss you all. Please let [my son] know that I put in a special word for him with Santa, never stop believing because if you can't believe you can't live. I love all of you and miss you terribly. Merry Xmas kids, Love Dad.*

Shortly after Christmas, Brian wrote again, this time expressing his gratitude for the giving spirit of those back home…because it was that spirit that was aiding in their safety:

Good Morning from Afghanistan! While you were all sleeping a great group of soldiers from Britain, and your very own Air Force, Army, Navy and Marines were busy doing a medical outreach for the local Afghan people. While we truly are humbled by what we get to see and do, we also know how important this job is. If we do it well and keep the local people happy, it directly correlates with a significant decrease in the amount of times we get bombed. So, even though we didn't know it,[the shipments of clothing and food] you are providing are very serious and a needed service to all of us over here and WE ALL THANK YOU.

Today was a beautiful morning with about 2 inches of snow on the ground from the day before and rather warm with a high of 41 degrees. What began as a white beautiful morning at an Afghan schoolhouse, ended up a muddy yet successful day. While I can't show every piece of clothing that you have sent, I am sending you a series of photos of what was accomplished today. All of you through your gifts of kindness, prayers and support are what made today and every day spent as a soldier here worthwhile.

Today I learned a very valuable lesson. While the photos show you smiling children (sometimes) and people with your gifts of kindness, it is war out here. These folks will push, shove, spit, drop their little ones; kick, steal, and I swore I saw kickboxing as well today. Usually we are in buildings and can control access in and out of an area, but today it was an open air event; this is no joke, adults will steal from the kids and men from the women. That is just the way it is here, but I've been getting sneakier. Now I make them put it on or they don't get it. That way it is harder to rip off, but sometimes they squeak by without anyone noticing that they took something.

Just for my medical cronies, you should all join the military and come over. You get the opportunity to practice medicine without ANY paperwork out here and you practice your art while sporting a weapon. Occasionally you get shot at and bombed, but where else can you practice outside and get run over by an angry mob wanting articles of clothing? I know you wish you were here and I've seen things where I wish you were here too.

Brian went on to thank everyone for their kindness, their prayers and support. Every day Brian looked for the good. It was his way of staying grounded and infusing a bit of peace into those back at home.

TIP: There is humor and good in most every situation. Gravitate toward the positive. You do have a choice in what you focus on.

Keeping Your Worlds Connected

Fortunately, there are many ways to stay connected to your spouse while you or your spouse is deployed. Modern day technology (i.e. Internet, IM, cell phone, etc) as well as old-fashioned letter writing make the distance between the worlds seem shorter. Jody and Brian worked their schedules to IM (instant message) on a frequent basis. Mike purchased a cell phone and airtime cards so that he could call his wife and when he had a moment, he would write. Essentially, every couple I spoke with found ways to keep connected; when they chose to.

Dr. Bridgett Cantrell, leading psychologist and author of the acclaimed post traumatic stress disorder book, *Downrange to Iraq and Back* shared with me that it is absolutely vital that [military] families find ways to communicate. In her words, *communication, communication, communication is so very important.*

Tonia and Mike essentially started their own letter writing campaign. *Keeping the connection alive was relatively easy. I am a talker and am very good at it. So everything I would tell him I just put on paper. My co-workers were baffled at how much I could write but with two toddlers what could I not write about?* And Mike responded. As a matter of fact, Mike managed to write his son six letters, Tonia thirty seven and his daughter one hundred and thirty nine. Mike couldn't bear talking to his daughter, but he had no challenge writing her. And he did it so that she would always have something to read and reflect back on in the event he didn't come home.

Jody had her sons write letters sharing how they did at school or what they were feeling and then she'd scan them and send them via email. Brian wanted to be in the loop regarding the boys' successes and challenges and he wanted to be able to provide direction and advice. He took the time to make a video for one of his sons congratulating him on an award he received. Brian wasn't going to allow distance to stand in the way of providing Father Power, praise and encouragement. And because Brian had no phone, IM and email was his only source of communication outside of letter writing. For Jody letter writing was way too slow anyway.

Choosing NOT to Disconnect

Technology allows soldiers and their families to stay better connected than any other time in history. With the ease of staying connected it is also quite easy to disconnect. Because you and your spouse are no longer face to face, you become dependent on some form of technology that you can turn on – and off – at a whim. There's tremendous power in having the ability to control when you talk – and it can be addictive and dangerous.

When I sat with Brian and Jody, this was a major issue for Jody. They bantered back and forth throughout the interview about this issue of control and neither held back. To capture the feel of the interview, I left Jody's comments italicized and bolded Brian's responses:

*When it came to family, they [Brian and the other soldiers] were the ones in control. Brian would be like "Hmmm, I'll see if Jody is online today, or at this hour." And usually I was right there. **Waiting*** *for my beckon call. Oh my gosh, I haven't talked to Brian this hour; usually he's available. You know? And if he didn't feel like going on that day, he didn't go on. There was this day we got in a fight...an Internet fight. I kid you not. And I was like f**** you I'm not talking to you until Sunday. Deal with it.*

Four days Brian went about his business, disconnected from Jody and his kids. And Jody was absolutely powerless not knowing anything. She had no way to communicate with Brian until *he* decided it was time.

It is not unusual that the stress and pressure of the daily events, compounded by being separated, may cause you and your spouse to fight in ways that are foreign to your relationship. Historically, Brian was very vocal in his relationship with Jody. When he was deployed, Brian said he would disconnect:

because [he] could. The mentality is don't tell me about your insignificant f****** problems because I don't care. I have enough issues here; we just sent a boy home in a bag, so don't tell me about YOUR f****** problems.

But as Jody was quick to point out, she and others just didn't see it that way. Disconnecting was never part of their relationship and to Jody her problems were very significant.

We don't see that. We see that we are raising their children, trying to make men out of these boys and they [the boys] won't, you know, they won't take

*the time to help us do the dishes – they won't help
with anything because we're being a mean mom
and they only listen to dad; and Brian chose to go
over and be a part of this...and he [Brian] doesn't
want to be bothered?*

When Brian decided he was ready to talk, Jody wasn't. So another day passed before they settled their argument. Fortunately, nothing happened to Brian or Jody that prevented them from bringing resolution to their issues.

TIP: You absolutely need to determine on the front end how you are going to work through disagreements...without disconnecting.

You and your spouse will experience different lives. One of you will struggle with keeping life the same back home, yet, your life at home won't be the same while your spouse is deployed. Events that never affected you, may affect you. If you have children, often, they won't understand the separation and you'll struggle with how to communicate. Every day will bring different emotions and challenges. Life back home will not stand still; it will move forward and you will change. That's okay.

One of you will find yourself in a world you never imagined. You may be required to put your life on the line...everyday. You will fight shutting home out and staying connected. You will have a routine and this routine will cause you to become "machine-like." You will change. And you will need to change again when you return home. Be prepared.

Bringing It Home

✯ ✯ ✯

Strategy #4 for strengthening your marriage:

Communication is a must do during your separation. The heart will grow fonder as you stay connected and be sure you keep your conversations encouraging. Your spouse is not to be used as a dumping ground.

Questions to consider:

1. What are things you can do to serve your spouse during deployment?

   _____

   _____

   _____

   _____

2. How will you work through the difficult moments to-gether?

   _____

   _____

   _____

   _____

3. Knowing you both will be changed by this experience, what will you do to grow closer through the changes?

_____

_____

_____

_____

Final Thought: *People run toward people who encourage, not discourage. Become your spouse's greatest supporter and encourager and this will strengthen your marriage bond.*

CHAPTER 5

Marriage Support

Resources designed to help the service members, their spouse and families.

Tonia lived between two major military installations and yet, she still knew very little about the resources available to her.

> *Mike was in the Army, okay. I live seven miles from a huge naval base, you'd think they'd link the two even though yes you are a reservist... you are still activated;[you'd think they'd let you know that] your closest base is here, here's all the things we have to offer you; because I could go on the base, I could drive on the base, it didn't matter if I was Army or not; but you'd think they'd have some system in your area that would let you know "here's what you have." There's nothing like "here's your nearest base, here's how you get to it, here's your nearest hospital...how to set up claims with the VA"...nothing.*

Transitioning from civilian life to military life can be an abrupt change. In civilian life, you know what to expect, for the most part. You have your routines, you know what resources are available to you and you pretty much know what to expect from those resources. As a soldier, you'll develop a routine rather quickly and many resources will be at your fingertips. If you are the spouse staying behind, your routines and resources will change. Some for the good and others...well those still have room for improvement.

The key to a successful transition will come from taking the time to figure out what resources you will need, how to access them, what paperwork needs to be filled out and the services you can expect from them – prior to deployment.

The purpose of this chapter is to provide information on resources that will benefit your marriage, offer information on health and finances and provide insight on how to comfort your children through deployment, just to name a few. This is not a complete and exhaustive list, but it is not meant to be. To provide a complete list – one that seems to be growing every month – would be extremely overwhelming and inefficient. This short list of resources will focus your efforts and reduce your research time.

A word of caution: each branch offers valuable resources specific to their branch but also ones that go beyond their branch borders. For this reason, I encourage you to read what resources are noted under every branch, as you will only broaden your knowledge of what is available.

Resource Starting Points

The government has done a superb job of consolidating the magnitude of available information into two specific areas: Military HOMEFRONT and Military OneSource. They also work closely with the National Military Family Association, an independent organization that focuses their efforts solely on the military family.

Military HOMEFRONT is the official Department of Defense web site for reliable Quality of Life information. It is designed to help troops and their families, as well as leaders connect service providers with military families. The web portal is the central, trusted, and up-to-date source for service members and their families to obtain information about all Department of Defense Quality of Life programs and services. This is a great starting point and resource in which to locate information on your topic of interest. Visit: www.militaryhomefront.dod.mil

Military OneSoure is another excellent example of the branches working together to provide a consolidated resource for soldiers and their family members. Military OneSource is provided by the Department of Defense at no cost to active duty, Guard and Reserve (regardless of activation status), and their families. This source provides information on where to find help with child care, how to manage your personal finances or where to find emotional support during deployments. Relocation information and resources needed for special circumstances can be found here as well.

Military OneSource is also an excellent resource to find a local counselor. Face-to-face counseling sessions focus on issues such as normal reactions to abnormal situations (e.g. combat), couples concerns', work/life balance, grief and loss, adjustment to deployment, stress management, and parenting. **Persons seeking counseling will receive up to six counseling sessions per issue at no cost to them.** To access a counselor in your local community, call a Military OneSource consultant directly. The Stateside number is 1-800-342-9647 and Overseas you can call collect 1-484-530-5908. There is someone ready to take your call 24/7. If you have Internet, visit: www.militaryone source.com User Id: military and Password: onesource. Service is available in CONUS as well as Hawaii, Alaska, U.S. Virgin Islands and Puerto Rico.

The **National Military Family Association** (www.nmfa. org) is an independent, non-profit association that was founded in 1969 and originally known at the Military Wives Association. NMFA is considered "The Voice for Military Families" and is dedicated to serving the families and service members through education, information, and advocacy. This organization has significant support at top levels of the Department of Defense and is the only organization whose sole focus is the uniformed services family.

The goal of the organization is to educate military families concerning their rights, benefits, and the services available to them. Their website is chock full of information about the Association, current issues of concern and links to other websites of interest to military families.

Strengthening Your Marriage

Each branch has their own program designed to offer support to their married and single military personnel. The services recognize and understand the importance of keeping the morale of the single and married soldiers strong and this typically falls under the supervisory leadership and discretion of the chaplains. Currently, there is a trend in all branches to set an example of healthy relationships from top down.

Most of the programs offered are marriage enrichment events and not counseling programs so if you are in need of marriage counseling, check with your unit chaplain or Military OneSource. Regardless of your circumstances there is always a benefit in getting a marriage tune-up either through counseling or participation in a marriage enrichment program.

Before diving into resources that are branch specific, there are a few programs worth mentioning that were developed outside the military realm but apply very much to all military services. Two are specific to marriage and one is geared toward coming home.

Marriage L.I.N.K.S.

The Marriage L.I.N.K.S. program was developed by DR. John Van Epp and is a part of his LIFECHANGERS series. As his website, www.nojerks.com states: *The program teaches couples how to be active relationship managers and work together to keep their relationship strong and resilient.*

The program uses the RAM (relationship attachment model) to help couples visualize their feelings of closeness and intimacy. The actual RAM card is simple and yet very effective. You can slide the bar up or down the scale to indicate to your spouse where you see your relationship in specific categories like: how well you KNOW each other, where you are with TRUST in your relationship, how RELIABLE you feel your spouse is, and where you see the COMMITMENT level in your relationship. It also provides an area to rate where you think INTIMACY falls in the relationship. When I met with one of the command chaplains, he spoke very highly of the program because it went beyond the standard lecture series. The program is excellent in that it provides an easy format for couples to follow and a fun visual that brings the issues to the table in a non-threatening way. In some ways, the RAM card is like the Pick Your Mood magnet card except with a very powerful message on the mood of your relationship.

The military has over 500 chaplains certified to coach and train military personnel on the benefits of this program. For those outside the military one can become certified to coach this program as well.

America's Family Coaches

Dr. Gary and Barb Rosberg, nationally known speakers and co-hosts of their own syndicated daily radio program, have developed a 4-part DVD series specifically for military couples. The series is designed to encourage, teach and strengthen the military marriage. It is ideal for couples or small groups, provides fun and entertaining stories as well as thought provoking marriage principles. Their book *6 Secrets to a Lasting Love,* accompanies the DVD series and both can be adapted for marriage retreats or for use by each spouse separately during deployment. The Rose Ceremony that is featured on the DVD, is especially moving. The DVD provides hope just by showing that other military families have taken the steps to strengthen their marriages, despite the emotions and difficulties of deployment.

The Rosberg's have written over a dozen books on marriage from the Christian perspective, often pulling in personal stories and offering wisdom that they have gained throughout their own 30 plus years of marriage. Regardless of your religious affiliation the principles are sound.

The series will help you tackle pertinent issues such as conflict resolution, finances, emotional intimacy, romance, sexual intimacy, and how to persevere through life's ups and downs. To learn more about the series or other materials, visit their website at: www.americasfamily coaches.com or www.drgaryandbarb.com.

Hearts Toward Home International

Dr. Bridgett Cantrell is the founder of Hearts Toward Home International, a non-profit charitable organization, which has been structured for the purpose of providing support. Hearts Toward Home Int'l offers counseling, training, educational classes, materials, re-integration and re-adjustment workshop/forums for military personnel (both active duty and veterans) and their families after war-time service.

Having specialized in trauma for several years, Dr. Cantrell's primary work now encompasses treating war veterans and their family members from all eras. She also works with those veterans who have been sexually abused while serving in the military.

The *Turning Your Heart Toward Home* workbook course and the self-help book *Down Range: To Iraq and Back* address the issues that deployed military personnel, as well as all war veterans, face upon re-entering society.

Down Range provides answers, explanations, and insights into why so many combat veterans suffer from flashbacks, depression, rage, nightmares, anxiety, emotional numbing, and other troubling aspects of Post-Traumatic Stress Disorder (PTSD). The true benefit of this book, which can be found at www.heartstowardhome.com is that it will share how to make healthy transitions from war to peace.

THE ARMY'S COMMITMENT TO MARRIAGE

The Army is committed to its soldiers and their families more so now than ever before. They understand that family support often means the difference between one staying in the service and one leaving. Because of this clear understanding, they are undergoing some of the most aggressive changes since WWII. As mentioned at www.Army.mil, *support for soldiers, civilians and their families are a critical part of the Army's ability to defend our Nation.*

Strong Bonds (www.strongbonds.org) is a truly valuable resource for single soldiers, couples and families. The two day program, in which you and your spouse are flown to the destination and housed at no expense to you in a nice hotel, is designed to empower soldiers and their families with relationship skills as well as provide an environment where one can learn how to build and maintain strong communication skills. As one chaplain shared, *just get them into marriage training and they will get benefit* is true. Over 30,000 Army couples have participated in Strong Bonds and more than 90 percent of those participants gave the program a positive rating.

As a deployed service member, as long as your unit chaplain implements the program, you can attend in-theater while your spouse participates back at home.

Strong Bonds is committed to the restoration and preservation of Army families and serves as a connection point for community health and support resources. The website is loaded with information on how to preserve and strengthen relationships as well as how to participate in the program. This is one resource you and your spouse will definitely want to research and determine when you should participate.

The **Army Reserve Family Programs** (www.arfp.org) also known as MyArmyLifetoo.com is committed to offering education, training, awareness, outreach, information, referral, and follow-up for Reservists and their families. Their message is simple: SR + FR =MR; or for those not quite caught up on military acronyms: Soldier Ready (SR) plus Family Readiness (FR) equals Mission Readiness (MR).

The site is packed with information and links to various programs and resources that range from Benefits, to Child and Youth Services, Counseling Assistance, Finances, Family Readiness and Post Deployment Counseling.

There are many other useful services and programs noted on the site as well, so if you are a family member of a Reservist, this site should definitely be marked as a "favorite."

THE NAVY'S COMMITMENT TO MARRIAGE

"Mission Readiness through Family Readiness" is the mission statement for the Navy Reserve. It's not uncommon for sailors and their families to experience long deployments; as a matter of fact, there has been a long history of sailors being deployed months on end in order to satisfy the mission. So in some ways, the Navy has a jump on how to handle long deployments. However, what is a bit uncommon is the new found stress and anxiety surrounding the deployments. As proven by the attack on the USS Cole, the Navy is not impervious to being a target and as a result, like the other branches, the Navy has devoted considerable time and money preparing their sailors and making improved resources available to spouses and other family members.

The Navy has done a superb job in compiling information and resources at http://navyreserve.navy.mil/Public/ HQ/welcomeaboard/CNRFC+Families. One of the most beneficial links on this site is the *Guard and Reserve Benefits Guide*. This link will take you to the DoD's *Taking Care of America's Armed Forces Families*. The 21 page guide includes recent changes in law and policy so you have the most current information on military benefits and privileges. The guide identifies a number of benefits regardless of your service affiliation. It covers the eligibility requirements of the benefits and most importantly identifies where you can get assistance when you have specific questions and problems. Any questions regarding family issues can be emailed to CNRFCFAMILIES@Navy.Mil or you can call 1-866-830-6466. **This is an extremely beneficial resource and although not specific to marriage, it will aid in relieving some anxiety...which is always helpful to a marriage.**

Another great resource, provided by the Commander of the Navy Installations Command, is **The Navy Fleet and Family Support Center** (www.nffsp.org). NFFSP provides family-focused programs and services designed to support long deployments and improve Navy readiness. The programs offered are also geared toward strengthening the individual and their family.

The site is diverse in that it offers information on Individual Augmentees (IA), Ombudsman Programs, Deployment Readiness and Family Advocacy. The Navy has also made finding a local or regional command simple with *The Family Center Locations* link. Whether you are stationed overseas or in the United States, finding the contact information for your region is made simple.

The most noteworthy link is the *Families* link. It provides information on what programs are available on the issues that affect the sailor and his or her family members the most. *Money Matters, Employment, Personal Counseling* and *Parenting in a Military Family* are some of the links worth exploring.

The Navy's **CREDO program,** originally known as the Chaplains Religious Enrichment Development Operation, is now known as the Spiritual Fitness Division. The Navy has successfully helped couples maneuver through family issues for more than 35 years. The sponsored retreat program helps improve job performance and enhance the quality of life for active-duty members and their families. It is not designed as a marriage counseling program but more of a marriage enrichment/improvement program.

To take advantage of or gather more information on some of the programs and services, you'll want to contact your local Ombudsman.

THE AIR FORCE'S COMMITMENT TO MARRIAGE

The Air Force Personnel Center, located at Randolf AFB, is devoted to providing information on all aspects of life in the Air Force. When you visit http://ask.afpc.randolph.af.mil you will find answers for many of your questions. With regard to family issues and support services, visit the *Personnel Services* link at the top of the site and in the drop down box you'll see the *Family Support Services* option. This will direct you to the Air Force's Family Matters Operations web page. Most, if not all, of your questions can be answered here or you can email your question to AFCRO@randolph.af.mil: the site recommends you visit your local Family Support Center or the Military Homefront website. Both will be able to direct you on what is available to improve your marriage.

The "Official Community Website of the United States Air Force," Air Force Cross Roads, is found at www.afcrossroads.com. Like the other branch services sites, AF Crossroads offers tips on how to cope with all phases of deployment, offers an online application for *Family Subsistence Supplemental Allowance*, which can be found under the *Financial Information* link, covers *Parenting* issues as well as *Health and Wellness*. This last link houses information on medical and dental, fitness and nutrition, TRICARE and Stress Management just to name a few. The suggestions and tips under each one of these categories is helpful. The information provided is just a teaser but it does offer sound suggestions.

Just knowing that you are not alone in what you are experiencing can be quite helpful in maintaining some sort of balance in your relationships. AF Crossroads has a link to their *Spouse Network* which offers advice from your peers on practically everything; kids, pets, family, etc... This registered access site is a great place to seek referrals if you are looking for professional counseling or advice.

Overall, your best place to start for marriage related issues is your local Family Support Center or www.AirforceOne Source.com which will redirect to MilitaryOneSource.

THE MARINES COMMITMENT TO MARRIAGE

It is said that to be a Marine you are part of an elite team... the few, the proud, the Marines. Once a Marine, always a Marine is not just a cute saying. This belief extends to family as well. While it isn't easy to become a Marine nor is the job of a Marine easy, what is not so well known is the understanding by many that to be *married* to a Marine is one of the toughest jobs of the Corps.

Lt. General Lewis B. "Chesty" Puller, USMC, one of the most decorated and well respected Marines summed up the attitude of a Marine, "All right, they're on our left, they're on our right, they're in front of us, they're behind us... they can't get away this time." Marines are known to tackle challenges face on; after all, they are known for securing the beach fronts so others can safely move forward. This attitude works fine on the battlefield but this calculated and cold approach isn't necessarily so great in a marriage.

Fortunately, a Marine can take advantage of what is offered by both the Corps and the Navy. As a Marine there are many resources available to help you strengthen your family.

When you start at the Marine Corps website www.usmc.mil you will notice at the top of the page a tab for *Family*. This link will provide several options, one being *Marine Corp Family Team Building*. This site is an excellent resource page and you can access it directly by going to www.usmc-mccs.org/family. Information on Dr. John Van Epp's L.I.N.K.S. program can be found here in addition to CREDO and one of the military's most prized programs, PREP.

PREP, an acronym for **Prevention & Relationship Enhancement Program**, has been featured on 20/20, 48 Hours, and Oprah because of its straight-forward approach to teaching skills one needs to better nurture a lasting and loving relationship. The program is designed to prepare and enrich your relationship and NOT as a counseling or therapy program to provide one on one marriage coaching.

The Navy chaplain's network, www.chaplaincare.navy.mil, supports the Marine Corps and the Coast Guard. Navy chaplains are prepared to deal with the challenges faced by service members from a number of different angles. The *USMC* link offers information on what services to contact regarding Domestic Violence, Child Abuse, Marine Deployment as well as phone numbers for the Marine Corps Family Referral Hotline.

Bringing It Home

Strategy #5 for strengthening your marriage:

Military OneSource is still your best resource for marriage counseling, outside of a referral or your unit chaplain. Take the time to know what is offered by your service branch and what you can take advantage of outside of your service branch. There's no question that most of you serving, whether actively or emotionally, are proud of your involvement; be proud enough of your marriage to seek the right coaching, mentorship and counseling that will help clear a path to greater heights in your marriage.

Questions to consider:

1. How far are you from the nearest military installation? What resources and programs are made available to you or your spouse at this installation?

_____

_____

_____

_____

_____

_____

2. What is your action plan to manage your marriage through this time of service?

_____

_____

_____

_____

_____

3. What marriage enrichment program or resource have you and your spouse discussed and decided to participate in?

_____

_____

_____

_____

4. At what point will you attend this program?

_____

_____

_____

_____

5. List the outside resources you have identified to help you and your spouse through some of the difficult times?

_____

_____

_____

_____

_____

_____

_____

Final Thought: *Too much information can be disabling; not knowing where to turn can be frightening. Take control. There is comfort in searching for specific answers and seeking help. There is infinite strength and courage that comes into your relationship when you find those answers.*

CHAPTER 6

Understanding Health Care, Counseling and Finances

Making the complicated simple

The issues surrounding health care and finances play heavily on a marriage. Naturally, every family situation will be different. Some may have all these details worked out and some may be struggling to make ends meet. Prior to Brian's deployment, he worked *six frickin' jobs,* as he said, just to maintain and support his financial and medical coverage needs. To an outsider his life would appear chaotic; to him there was a delicate balance. When he was deployed, that balance was interrupted. Fortunately, Brian worked aggressively on the front end to make the transition as smooth as possible for Jody and their children.

But what if your life is like the majority of people where the chaos of daily living has you running around putting out small fires? And now you have the issue of deployment. Who has time to understand all the benefits, counseling and financial stuff? Tons of paperwork are shoved your direction and the simple fact is that it is easier to ignore all of it or just sign it versus understanding it.

The purpose of this chapter is to provide some baseline understanding of the services that will bring tremendous benefit.

TRICARE MEDICAL

As a member of the military community, whether active duty (and this includes activated Guard and Reserves), re-tiree or family member, one of the benefits you are entitled to is the Department of Defense's comprehensive health care program TRICARE. This massive health care system is designed to bring together the resources of the DoD and supplement them with a network of civilian health care professionals.

The result provides beneficiaries between the ages of 0 to 64 with three options: TRICARE Prime, TRICARE Extra and TRICARE Standard. The basics are covered below but for an in-depth explanation of TRICARE benefits visit www.tricare.mil.

TRICARE Prime

As an active duty service member, you must enroll in TRI-CARE Prime. Your beneficiaries are also eligible for this program and can choose to enroll. It is important to note that if your spouse has an employer-sponsored health plan, review your options and determine whether TRICARE will be of benefit. One of the features of the TRICARE site is the *Plan Wizard*. This feature allows you to input your information and determine which plan will best suit you and your family.

If you determine that TRICARE is a viable option, be sure to enroll. You must fill out and submit the enrollment forms to the regional contractor or to the nearest military treatment facility (MFT) before you can take advantage of the benefits.

TRICARE Prime offers service members the most affordable and comprehensive coverage of all the plans. Another excellent feature to the plan is that it does not require an enrollment fee. It does require you to enroll, but it does not require you to pay to enroll.

Plan Features

This plan is made available to:

1. Active duty service members and their families.
2. Retired service members and their families under the age of 65.
3. Eligible former spouses under the age of 65.
4. National Guard and Reserve members and their families when the National Guard or Reserve member is activated for more than 30 consecutive days.
5. Medal of Honor recipients and their families.

With TRICARE Prime, most of your health care services will come from the MTF. When those services aren't readily available, you will see one of the contracted Civilian Medical Providers in the Preferred Provider Network.

There are a few key features that make this option one to strongly consider:

1. There are fewer out-of-pocket costs than other TRI-CARE options.
2. You have enhanced coverage for vision and clinical preventive services
3. There are no claims to file (in most cases).

Although there are many benefits to this plan, of which you can view the extensive list at www.tricare.mil there are a few disadvantages to be aware of:

1. Your provider choice is limited.
2. Any specialty care is by referral only.
3. The plan is not universally accepted. Be sure the plan is accepted in your region.

Click on the *Compare Plans* link to examine side by side comparisons of TRICARE plans and their coverage. A cost comparison of the plans can be found at www.military.com/benefits/tricare/tricare-prime/tricare-prime-overview.

TRICARE Extra

With TRICARE Extra, you don't have to enroll or pay an annual fee in order to take advantage of this plan. Like Prime, there is no enrollment fee; however, you do have to satisfy an annual deductible for out-patient care. If you are familiar with insurance in the civilian marketplace, this plan is much like a Preferred Provider Option (PPO). It is important to note that TRICARE Extra is not available overseas or to active duty service members.

This plan is geared toward:

1. Active duty family members.
2. Retirees and their family members under age of 65.
3. Survivors and eligible former spouses under 65.
4. Family members of National Guard or Reserve members who are activated for more than 30 consecutive days.

When you receive care from a TRICARE Extra network provider, you get a discount on cost sharing and you don't have to file your own claims. Like Prime, the issue of endless paperwork is eliminated in this plan.

A few key advantages to Extra:

1. No balance billing.
2. No deductible when using a retail pharmacy network.
3. No forms to file.
4. TRICARE Extra may be used on a case-by-case basis.

A few key disadvantages to Extra:

1. Provider choice is limited.
2. Requires payment of deductibles and co-payments.
3. The plan is not universally accepted.

TRICARE Standard

TRICARE Standard is the military's fee-for-service option that provides beneficiaries the chance to see any TRICARE authorized provider. The plan is designed to be extremely flexible but with this flexibility comes higher out-of-pocket costs. This is not a "save you time and money" plan, as it will require filing claims and other such paperwork. However, under this plan TRICARE Extra is also made available.

Like Extra, the plan is geared toward the same beneficiaries and is not available to active duty service members. The true benefit to the plan is its flexibility and its worldwide availability.

A few key advantages to Standard:

1. The freedom to choose from any TRICARE-authorized provider.
2. Available worldwide.
3. No enrollment process.
4. You may use TRICARE Extra.

A few key disadvantages to Standard:

1. The highest out-of-pocket costs.
2. PAPERWORK. Beneficiaries may have to do their own paperwork and file their own claims.
3. You pay the balance if the bill exceeds the allowable charges.

TRICARE Dental

The TRICARE Dental program (TDP) was implemented February 1, 2001 and is a voluntary, premium-based insurance program made available to active duty family members, members of the National Guard and Reserve and family members of National Guard and Reserve members.

To find out if you are eligible for the program, visit the TRICARE website and click on *Dental.* You can also visit www.TRICAREdentalprogram.com or call toll free (800)866-8499 24 hours a day to obtain more information on enrollment.

The program is administered by United Concordia Companies, Inc (www.ucci.com) and they make available on their website a complete benefits and cost share fact sheet. If you have challenges navigating this site, go to www. military.com, click on *Benefits*, then *TRICARE* and select *Dental*; they also provide a side-by-side cost comparison.

Veteran Benefits

When you leave active duty, you do not lose all your benefits. As a veteran you, and in most cases your family members, become eligible for benefits provided through the Department of Veterans Affairs. The VA provides a medical health package to all enrolled veterans that emphasize preventive and primary care. A full range of inpatient and outpatient services are made available through the VA health care system.

When you visit their website, www.va.gov, click on the *Health Care* link and then navigate to the *Health Benefits & Services* link. The site offers detailed information on health care benefits, where to find a facility, how to get prescriptions filled as well as a suicide hotline. Information on a number of health-related programs are also listed.

The Department of Veterans Affairs Health Administration Center (HAC), based out of Denver, administers the federal health benefits programs for all veterans and their family members. Their vision is to promote the health and well being of veterans and their families. Visit the *CHAMPVA* link to fill out the application for CHAMPVA benefits.

COUNSELING

The events and emotions derived from war are not an individual issue but a family issue. Steve Akers, who served in Vietnam and has since been counseling veterans and their families for over twenty two years, firmly advocates that counseling is a family issue.

When Steve was discharged from Vietnam, his thoughts raced from *why am I not a cowboy anymore* to *I don't belong here*, referring to home. The issues he sees today are similar to the issues many veterans saw coming out of Vietnam. Families are often shattered by back to back tours, the spouse who remains at home becomes extremely independent, the kids don't "know" dad or mom, the service member doesn't really know how to fit in…bottom line, there is a lot of emotional turmoil and strain.

They flat out struggle with readjusting. It's for these reasons Steve sees many of the service members willing to return to battle.

But there is hope and help. Steve and many other trained professionals have committed their lives to helping men and women who have served our country – as well as their family members – walk through these issues. The government has also taken measures to establish programs and resources for the service member as well as family members who seek assistance. Check with your chaplain or Military OneSource.

So whether you call it counseling or coaching, getting qualified help is a sign of strength and not weakness. When you do this, you reaffirm your commitment to improving yourself, your marriage and your family. The tough part will be taking the first steps – agreeing or accepting that you need help and then taking action.

Understanding PTSD

Working through Post Traumatic Stress Disorder (PTSD) is one of the most frequently mentioned hurdles facing our service members. This debilitating disorder can affect anyone who has experienced a life threatening or traumatic event and it is becoming a more common occurrence for those who serve in Iraq and Afghanistan. According to a 2004 Department of Defense study published in the New England Journal of Medicine, 17 percent of American soldiers who served in Iraq suffered from some sort of major depression, generalized anxiety or Post Traumatic Stress

Disorder. The DoD estimates between 15 – 29 percent of veterans from the wars in Iraq and Afghanistan will suffer from PTSD. It is important to understand what the symptoms are and where to seek help.

The National Center for PTSD (www.ncptsd.va.gov) is recognized as the world's leading expert on Post Traumatic Stress Disorder. This organization has thoroughly studied the symptoms, treatments and therapies and is a resource for those who need help. They have 7 divisions devoted to understanding the issues important to American veterans and they continue developing methods to improve veterans' overall well-being. **It is important to note that NCPTSD does not provide direct clinical care or individual referrals.** However, this website does provide invaluable information to better understand the symptoms of PTSD, treatments used to combat it and locate the nearest facility where care is provided.

The site will give you guidance on issues to consider when selecting a therapist as well as where to find a support group. To better understand your coverage for individual and family care, contact Veterans Affairs at 1-800-827-1000.

Vet Centers

Out of recognition that a significant number of Vietnam vets were still experiencing readjustment issues, Congress, in 1979, established the Vet Center Program. The Centers, which number over 200 and are located in all 50 states, provide a broad range of counseling and outreach services to ALL veterans who served in a combat zone. Their main focus is helping veterans make a satisfying post-war readjustment back into civilian life.

Vet Centers (www.vetcenter.va.gov) are staffed by teams of dedicated and qualified providers. Many are combat veterans themselves who provide guidance to others who are experiencing what they experienced. If you or your loved one is having challenges making the transition, this is a great place to start looking for assistance.

In 2003, the Vet Centers began offering bereavement counseling services to surviving parents, spouses, children and siblings of service members who died while on active duty. This now includes the federally activated Reserve and National Guard.

One of the most noteworthy benefits is, since its inception in 1979, family members of combat veterans have been eligible for readjustment counseling. As Alfie Ramos, Deputy Director for Washington State Department of VA said, *there is not such thing as "normal" and upon return, the service member needs to sit down with the family and talk about their feelings and needs to ensure the whole family understands and works through the issues...together.* Counseling is a family issue, and the Vet Centers honor this belief. To locate your nearest Vet Center, go to the Vet Center website, click on *Vet Center National Directory* and then highlight your state. You can also call toll free 1-800-905-4675 (Eastern) or 1-866-496-8838 (Pacific) during normal business hours and someone will be available to assist.

The Department of Veterans Affairs is serious about helping service members make a positive transition back into
civilian life. They know the sacrifice, the pain and the uncertainty that comes with serving our country during war
time; and for these reasons, there is no cost for Vet Center
readjustment counseling. Vet Centers provide a safe environment for healing to take place.

Children's Counseling

According to a recent UCLA study, the Department of
Defense estimates there are approximately 1.2 million
school-age kids whose parents are on active duty. There
is no official count of how many of these children have a
deployed parent.

Cheryl and Jody agreed that one of the biggest struggles they faced throughout their husbands' deployment
was how to comfort their children. To Cheryl, having
her children, ages fourteen, eleven, nine, six and four in
counseling was a blessing. Cheryl admitted her kids were
"basket cases." It is no wonder that the media has widely
repeated that war's developing casualty is military kids;
especially those children who are not accustomed to the
military lifestyle.

If you have children, consider getting them involved with
a qualified counselor. The emotional anxiety caused by
you or your spouse being deployed may stay dormant for
some time. And then it surfaces. Tonia shared that she
and Mike still struggle with helping their daughter cope

with Mike's deployment. Even though Mike survived, has been home for two years and is actively involved with his family, "Sam," their daughter, struggles with the issue of death. She is absolutely terrified with thoughts of losing her daddy; so much so that she recently brought home a picture of her daddy standing in a grave surrounded by tombstones.

To have a qualified adult who isn't stressed out by the situation take the time to listen, provide guidance and relate to your child will make a measurable difference in the attitude and well-being of your children for years to come.

Call your **Installation Family Support Center** to ask for a list of free counseling options available to your children.

To find a qualified counselor or therapist, you can always call **Military OneSource** (1-800-342-9627) for area referrals. In addition, your TRICARE regional contractor will likely be able to provide a list of area network counselors. Counseling and therapy can range from $5 at a community mental health center to well over $150 an hour for a private therapist. It is your responsibility to know whether your insurance covers mental health services, so be sure you check with TRICARE, if in fact this is your insurance, or with your private carrier first.

Children's Books

Children (and adults) will often turn to books for entertainment. But while being entertained, they can be educated and comforted. The site www.militaryfamilybooks.com offers many great resources for both adults and children affected by family members who are deployed. A portion of the profits go toward programs that support military families.

FINANCES

The services are aware that deployment can cause a tremendous burden on families not only emotionally but financially, so they've established programs and subsidies to relieve some of the stress.

Financial Aid for Child Care

In Cheryl's situation, when Peter deployed she was able to stay at home so child care wasn't an issue – except when she needed relief. Family members would often step in and provide a moment of relief so Cheryl could gain some sanity. But what if this isn't your situation? What if your situation requires you to seek outside work just to stay solvent and now the prospect of having to seek child care and find the money to cover it is a cause for anxiety?

The military's program for child care is highly praised for its quality and affordability and is quickly becoming a model for the entire nation. In 2007, the **National Association of Child Care Resource and Referral Agencies** (www.naccrra.org) rated the DoD child care program number one in the nation for its standards and oversight. No individual program received a higher rating.

Here's what is so great about this organization. The NAC-CRRA works closely with the DoD to help those who serve in the military find affordable child care. When you visit the NACCRRA website, you'll see the link *Supporting our Nation's Military Families and Strengthening Child Care*; click on the link and you'll find the four major branches are represented and each one offers a link to a *Military Subsidy Application*. The site provides a clear list of documents you'll need to submit with your application.

Additionally, you will find a link to *Operation: Military Child Care* outlining what financial assistance is available for activated or deployed National Guard and Reserve who have children enrolled in non-DoD licensed child care. To learn more visit www.childcareaware.org, which is part of NACCRRA, or call 1-800-424-2246.

NACCRRA will also do the legwork necessary to locate qualified child care in your neighborhood if you are not near a military installation. This is often the case with Reserve and Guard members. The Department of Defense recognizes this issue, among others, and has put stop gap measures in place to provide relief and assistance.

Financial Emergencies

Financial emergencies are not reserved for just those in the military. If you are experiencing some sort of financial strain, understand that there are many who are in the same situation. Not that this point really brings you comfort. If the ship you are on is sinking, does it really make you feel any better that there are dozens more on board that will go down with you? Probably not. Just know that financial issues can hit anyone, regardless of their affiliation with civilian life or military life. Whether you still get the paper delivered to your door step or read it online, you most likely encounter articles that feature families or companies that are experiencing financial trouble.

Because of the commonality, **Military OneSource** (this site is worth mentioning again) has devoted an entire section of their website to address *Money Matters*. This section covers everything from budgeting, home buying, credit and collections, to saving and investing and of course, taxes. They also make available information on *Emergency Financial Resources*. Aside from articles and web links, Military OneSource provides a guide that details additional resources to support families during military deployment. You will need to register and create a login with www.MilitaryOneSource.org before you can view and download the guide.

In the unfortunate event that you or your spouse was injured, or your spouse died in the line of duty, the 9-11 HelpAmerica Foundation (www.911helpamerica.com), a non-profit 501 c3, may be able to provide assistance. Injury and death often cause tremendous financial burdens in addition to emotional anxiety. The goal of HAF is to locate and help military families or individuals who have been affected by the wars and try to help them through direct donations.

Truly, there are hundreds of organizations and resources made available to ease many of the challenges faced by today's military families. If you have the time, visit **America Supports You** (www.americasupportsyou.mil), click on *Servicemembers* and you'll find more than 150 non-profit organizations that are dedicated to helping you and your family members.

BRINGING IT HOME

★ ★ ★

Strategy #6 for strengthening your marriage:

Accept help. Know that you are not alone and that you can make it individually and as a couple through your situation with the right mentorship and counseling.

Questions to consider:

1. Are you familiar with what your medical plan covers? If not, begin to understand it.

_____

_____

_____

_____

2. Have you listed the benefits counseling would have in your life and your family's life? If not, consider doing so.

_____

_____

_____

_____

3. What have you done financially to prepare for additional counseling or health care costs should the need arise?

_____

_____

_____

4. Have you set aside time so that your child or children can "just talk" about whatever is on their mind?

_____

_____

_____

5. Do you have a "rainy day" fund? If not, have you explored the resources made available to you in case of a financial emergency? List your top three:

1. _____

2. _____

3. _____

Final Thought: *The most powerful thing about mentorship and resources is using them. Remember, the man or woman at the top – financially, spiritually, emotionally and in his or her marriage – didn't fall there.*

CHAPTER 7

Keeping Your Marriage Strong

"Commitment is just that: commitment,
for better and for worse."

Understanding Marriage

Challenges are a part of marriage. Sometimes being married is flat out painful. According to Army Chaplain Alford, "marriages face challenges that have nothing to do with deployment." Do not think your challenges are unique. Marriage challenges are universal and don't discriminate. Chaplain Alford elaborated, "You take any two people, put them together and they'll have certain challenges." Just keeping a marriage together is a feat these days. Keeping *quality* in your marriage throughout deployment and after is absolutely impressive. And possible.

Do you remember how your relationship was formed? It's no wonder why keeping a marriage together is a herculean feat. Keri and I are like most couples; through some divine happenstance or mysterious coincidence we found each other, worked like heck to impress each other (I definitely had to work harder at impressing), promised each other the moon, were on our best behavior and then bound the relationship. Of course, I'm leaving out some details, but you get the point the "for better and for worse" had started.

Then the worse showed up AFTER the wedding. But maybe the worse was always there, just hiding behind cute and adorable? Now the small things, like leaving the top off the toothpaste or the lack of toilet paper in the bathroom at the most critical time – those habits we once thought were cute and could overlook, were now down right irritating. The quick temper, the sarcasm, the lack of accountability …where was all that during the courting?

Now you throw in a deployment. The Rand study, a study conducted by the National Defense Research Institute, recently reported that their subject couples felt that deployments are the most stressful part of military life. Chaplain Alford, a counselor for hundreds of couples and celebrant of dozens of weddings, backed this up: *even though the challenges can be universal in all marriages, the stages of deployment do compound the challenges for military couples.*

There are some positives of deployment. Those small things that started as cute and adorable, and then transformed into down right irritating tend to transform back to cute and adorable again. But then you wonder if there is anything you left undone or things left unsaid. The fact is you don't have your spouse by your side and you can't help but second guess yourself. What began as tough becomes incredibly difficult not only because of the thousands of geographical miles but the infinite emotional miles. How do you strengthen a relationship that may have started out weak and now has the added weight of deployment? Making it through these moments was described as having a barbell pressed against your chest with heavy weights on each side. You either press through it or get crushed. *You hold on to the vision – that perfect, romantic marriage picture in your head – and you focus on that...*

When I asked Jody to share how she, from her perspective, kept her marriage with Brian strong, she first explained the struggle. *You can't help but think 'what am I doing wrong?' There were constantly more negatives than positives – (with the kids) had to be the good guy and the bad guy...all the time. There is no one to relieve you...I couldn't even go to the store just to get a gallon of milk by myself. I was mad!* Jody laughed after she shared all this and then with absolute conviction said, *I got over it.*

Granted, Jody is a woman of strength. She is strong in her convictions, does not negotiate with her four kids and she got over it because she gave herself no exit. She made it through some of the rough moments because she romanticized her marriage and Brian...and then she'd talk to Brian on the phone and, well, so much for the romance. There were moments of hope that gave her the fuel to press forward.

After listening to so many couples share their stories, it was apparent that the fuel to press forward often came from their own personal commitment to their marriage vision and from their support network. Whether deployed or left behind they looked for ways to strengthen and support their commitment and not for reasons to give up. Support to get up or give up is readily available depending on where you seek your support. But as Tonia mentioned, *she did what she had to do* to make situations work because in her mind what other choice did she have? She had found support from a small network of ladies and God. For Tonia, she was rooted in her belief that *God does not lead you to a challenge unless He shows you a way through the challenge.* In some ways it's almost a Darwinian attitude: give up and go away or get strong and stay.

No one is suggesting you stay in an abusive or life threatening relationship. If that is your situation, you must seek immediate help and safety. It is only recommended that relationships currently faced with what may seem like insurmountable challenges created by circumstances in life commit to the decision to make it. Throughout the chapters of this book you've been provided insight into how others set their course, tackled some of the emotional issues and how they learned or benefited from their support networks and resources. Making it will come down to choosing to follow in the foot steps of other successful couples that have gone before you. The one thing left to make this work is your decision to make it work – and only *you* can make that decision.

Overcoming the Undertows

Sometimes it helps to understand what stands in the way of strengthening your relationship so you can prepare a work around. What ever you do don't dwell on the negative, as it has a way of finding tremendous support when given attention. But if you can at least understand what the common negatives are, then you can focus on their positive counterpoints and by doing so, you'll strengthen your relationship.

Perception vs. Reality

I think if you were to ask anyone on the street if deployment caused an increased risk of divorce for military couples, they'd likely say yes. Why? People struggle with their relationships when they're together, so it only makes sense that being apart adds to the struggle. A July 2006 New York Times article claimed "military deployments have a way of chewing up marriages, turning daily life upside down and making strangers out of husbands and wives." Partly true. Turning life upside is definitely true, but the February 2007 Rand Study suggests that "although the public associates deployments with high divorce rates, there is no direct evidence that deployments cause divorce." It's probably safe to assume deployments also don't strengthen a marriage, except to create a situation where the heart grows fonder if the relationship was healthy. What the study doesn't address is the quality of the relationships, as a result of deployment. It's one thing to stay married; it's another thing to be happily married and overcome complacency.

Overcoming Complacency

I was sitting in a coffee shop talking with one of my dear friends, Nebiye, when I saw a woman walk in and present the man who was sitting at the table next to me divorce papers. She took a seat, shoved a two inch stack of papers across the table and then they began addressing the issues. The conversation started civil, until the issue of their children came up and then it quickly spiraled... to the point Nebiye and I were thinking about moving tables.

From what I could unfortunately overhear, what started out as a torrid love relationship filled with promise, drifted quickly into complacency, failed expectations and eventually an affair. Their demise had nothing to do with deployment; if either had served, this was not the central point of their conversation. It had everything to do with losing sight of their original vision for their marriage. They allowed complacency, indecision and lack of accountability to permeate the bonds of their marriage. Expectations weren't met and when that happens distrust begins to build. With distrust come resentment, bitterness, judgment and perhaps even condemnation.

The validation for the negative is everywhere and that is when one begins to doubt love. Unfortunately, this isn't uncommon and as Chaplain Alford warned, "you'll face challenges that have nothing to do with deployment." Complacency, indecision and unaccountability are just a few you will have to safeguard against. Because of deployment, which compounds the issues, you will likely have to fight harder than most against these undertows to successfully cross the channel. If you don't, you'll join the couple at the coffee shop.

So what are the qualities of a healthy relationship? Dr. Kenneth Ackerman, who has also counseled hundreds of couples from all walks of life including couples in the military, points out "couples function well when they are able to freely give and receive love and trust in a healthy interdependent relationship." Meaning, there is equality in the relationship that serves the relationship. When the relationship creates a safe environment, built on trust and a desire to serve each other, self-serving behaviors are put aside. The issue of complacency becomes a non-issue and the attitude within the marriage is positive and not determined by circumstances. But is this whole attitude thing realistic in a deployment situation? It seems pretty common that both spouses insulate the other from events that are taking place on their front. So is a relationship separated by deployment truly forthcoming and able to *freely give and receive love?* *A*nd is it *a healthy interdependent relationship* despite the circumstances? Herein lays one of the largest challenges.

As Dr. Ackerman explained, "when one member in the relationship is called away, the sense of interdependence is broken. Both become very independent for survival. If the interdependence didn't change, there would be a great sense of emotional pain." This is one of the greatest marriage challenges you will face – the sense of interdependence being broken and you becoming independent in order to survive. And with independence comes a self-serving attitude. So what can you do?

First look for ways to uplift your spouse. Cheryl and Jody sent "fun" packages. You know, the type that reminds us husbands why we married our spouse in the first place. Brian emailed photos and personal video messages. Mike wrote letters. Numerous other couples seemed to follow the same path and utilized services and technology to keep the flame alive. This doesn't mean you necessarily sugar-coat everything; as Jody shared, she often didn't hold back in the emails – she'd let her anger fly, but she'd always end it with "I love you."

Dr. Ackerman offered these tips:

1. Work to keep the relationship based in a deep trust. Women can build this in their husbands by respecting the husbands. Men can do this by professing and showing their love. The book *Love & Respect* by Dr. Emerson Eggerichs explains how couples can establish their relationship in these two principles.

2. Wives need to feel secure. This security is emotional, financial, physical, and for religious couples, spiritual. When a wife doesn't feel secure, she will be distrustful. When she is distrustful of her husband or he is acting in a distrustful manner, it is difficult if not impossible to respect him.

Circumstances don't have to control the attitude within your marriage; but, because you are human, they most likely will influence your attitude. Self-doubt does creep in and at times the negatives seem to outweigh the positives. If you exercise your ability to build trust at every opportunity and find ways to uplift your spouse, you'll have a solid foundation from which to construct your post-deployment relationship.

Overcoming Indecision

If you've been married for any length of time, it's likely you suffer from decision constipation – the inability to make a decision on *anything*. You absolutely know you'd feel better if you could just get the decision out but the fear of making a wrong decision causes paralysis. You aren't alone. Most couples Dr. Ackerman sees in his practice suffer from this, or some variation of this which leads to unmet expectations. We provide little to no leadership in our relationships. If you think I'm kidding, the next time you are sitting with your spouse and he or she asks "what do you want to do," a gentleman's bet your spouse will answer, "I don't know, what do you want to do?" This question circles several more times before you decide to…watch TV. If you don't face this challenge you are ahead of the bell curve, but for most the spontaneity that runs rampant during the courtship often seems to fall victim to exhaustion and indecision in married life. If you are newly married and have no real history of living life together and your relationship is suddenly thrust into a deployment scenario, interdependence has little opportunity to gain traction and independence thrives; simply out of self-preservation. It's no easy task to make the decision that you'll make your relationship work, especially when all the issues have been magnified because of deployment.

Decisions are being made on a number of fronts. Once Mike deployed Tonia found herself having to make decisions on issues that were typically "Mike's department." She would run the important issues by Mike when she could, but ultimately, she made the decisions because often the issues needed immediate answers. It was the same with all the interviewed spouses who were left back home. Out of absolute necessity and survival, daily decisions were made with or without the deployed spouse's input. It is no different on the front line. Mike was making life and death decisions every day insuring his own survival with no input from Tonia. Both Tonia and Mike were making survival decisions…becoming *rulers of their own kingdoms or generals of their own world.* How they related to each other often came down to the decision to find a way to make a connection in their experiences. There is no room for indecision here. You will have to find ways to relate to your spouse.

If your marriage isn't healthy prior to deployment, you will face an uphill battle because of deployment. Any indecision to make your marriage work can be a death sentence to your relationship. When I asked Tonia if it was a fight to keep their marriage together, she answered *fight is definitely the word I would use.* They fought to keep their vision of life together alive.

1. Know and review your marriage vision. This will remove any indecision with regard to your marriage relationship.

2. Remind each other of the vision. There is a fine line here…don't nag. The "you said" thing doesn't work here. What I'm referring to is painting a picture of life together.

3. Decide that indecision will have no part in your relationship. Your checkpoint for this is how the decision or lack of decision fits in with your marriage vision.

4. Write letters. There is something nostalgic and seductive about writing letters…not emails, but letters. There is a certain amount of perceived romance that accompanies a letter. And with it, hope.

For Tonia, she badly wanted her marriage to be the same as it was when Mike left, so she wrote a lot of letters on her lunch break.

> *I wrote about anything and everything. I mostly kept my letters light and funny hoping they would be a pick-me-up. Mike has a great sense of humor so I would play some practical jokes on him through the mail and in turn he would play jokes on me. It was just a little part that seemed to keep 'my husband Mike alive' and not have him turn totally into the military soldier he was at the time.*

Overcoming indecision will only be countered by the amount of effort you put into making your marriage work, despite the circumstances. Look for ways to keep the hope and romance in your relationship. At one point in your relationship, you decided to bond your commitment. Go back to that day and write down why you made that decision.

Overcoming Unaccountability

Your accountability speaks to your character. It's about knowing who you are and what you stand for. For some of you, the issue of being accountable is not an issue. For others it is and if you don't pay attention to this attribute, it will cause tremendous challenges in your marriage. As mentioned, separation due to deployment causes an increase in stress on a relationship. If you are firm in knowing who you are, what you stand for and what value you place on your marriage, you'll overcome most if not all challenges your relationship will face. This starts with being accountable.

It's really not that hard, in concept. Do what you say you are going to do and stand by what you believe and you will be accountable. There is strength and security in accountability. We all know someone who, regardless of the circumstances or situations, stands firm in what he or she believes and always follows through with commitments. It goes without question why they seem to prosper in their relationships. We also know people who fail at this. Case in point: a friend of mine called the other day to set a lunch appointment. He does this often. I put it in my calendar…in pencil. I can count the number of times he has kept a lunch appointment on one hand; he commits to one thing and does another. He's accountable to being unaccountable. Yet, he never misses his early Monday morning basketball games.

We forget that our words and our actions reveal our character. What we tell our spouse, how we speak to our spouse, the vision we paint for our spouse either builds our relationship and creates trust inside the relationship or it tears at the very foundation we have built our relationship on and reveals the flaws in our character. Being accountable has nothing to do with distance or deployment. It has everything to do with character.

A Chaplain's Perspective

I spent several hours with Chaplain Alford, touring an army base, understanding some of the operations and the core programs made available to couples. It was readily apparent that when you are active duty, not the activated Reserve and Guard, but active duty in the sense that this is your chosen profession, there are a lot of family support programs available. The challenge comes in to play when you pull Reserve and Guard from across the country together to mobilize and form a unit. Suddenly, the support system for spouses becomes dependent on volunteers. At times it is very effective and others, like in Cheryl's case, it isn't. There can be a feeling of being *absolutely on your own*, especially if you are newly married.

This is where the chaplains play a large role. Every unit is assigned a chaplain or unit ministry team. Regardless of your religious beliefs, often their role is to provide a safe environment in which to share your concerns and find ways to help you strengthen your marriage. If you are the spouse who is manning the home front, you'll have a unit volunteer who is designated to assist in directing you to available resources. There is always support but sometimes you have to ferret it out.

There will be moments when you think "how can I – we – possibly survive this?" Chaplain Alford said for him there was comfort in knowing *God understands marriages and deployments.* He chose his role in the military because of his faith foundation and the opportunity to bring comfort to couples by sharing this belief and showing couples that throughout history soldiers have made it.

> *I read the Bible and I see many of God's people that were in deployments; military life is very much a part of the Old Testament, even in the New Testament. You have soldiers mentioned often – some very key passages and then the strongest statements...I think about marriage and marriage relationships come right there from the Bible.*

Chaplain Alford shares the above often with his troops. Even if you regard the Bible as nothing more than a history book, you'll see that soldiers and their families have survived deployments. They often struggled, but they survived. They survived because they believed in something bigger than themselves.

Roadmap to a Successful Marriage

There is wise counsel in learning from the mistakes of others, or following in the footsteps of someone who has successfully crossed the mine field. Chaplain Alford, after tours in Iraq, could relate to other soldiers who were experiencing marriage challenges and offer advice on how he and his wife made it through some of those same challenges. Outside of prayer, what truly worked for he and his wife was having a common goal for their marriage. He found that by working together toward a common goal, he and his wife stayed connected. You can do the same.

The disconnect happens when there are no common goals and the couple fails to seek help. Most marriage experts agree that struggling couples struggle because they don't ask for help before their situation becomes desperate. To avoid this, Dr. Ackerman suggests "couples need to be more willing to admit their struggles, their failures, their sorrows, as well as their pains and stop being cavalier or stoic." When they do this, they begin on the road to a healthy and successful marriage.

So where do you start on this roadmap to a successful marriage? Here are several suggestions:

1. Find a couple whom you respect and find out what they do to have the relationship they have. Because you respect this couple, there will be little embarrassment in seeking their advice and they will be honored you asked.

2. Identify common goals you want to achieve as a couple. Write these down and begin to explore how you can support each other in attaining the goals.

3. Find a marriage book you can work through together. This will begin the dialogue to uncovering some of the struggles, sorrows, pains and victories in both your personal life and your marriage.

4. Find a marriage coach. Every successful sports athlete has a coach. Have a marriage coach.

You will have to work at this. Success doesn't just happen. Negative happens without doing anything. Positive takes work.

Some suggestions on what other couples do to have successful marriages:

1. Think of the other person before you think of yourself. Look for ways to honor them in love and care.

2. Accept responsibility for dropping the ball when you do; and you will at times. We all fail and need to admit our mistakes.

3. Look for ways to build deeper interdependence. Each of you will be different and those differences will function like a division of labor. Where one is weak, the other can be strong. If you try to make your spouse like yourself, you are making one of you unnecessary.

4. Your spouse is your #1 priority over anything else… unless God is #1.

5. When making an apology for wrongs committed, also ask for forgiveness. Being forgiven is being given a clean slate. It does not condone the behavior or the fault, but it will help keep the bitterness and resentment from taking root in your heart.

The success of your relationship is going to be revealed in your daily habits. Those small decisions you make to speak words that either support and uplift or tear down and discourage will reveal your commitment to your marriage vision and the quality of your marriage relationship. Keeping your marriage strong requires you to manage your relationship. It only makes sense that to have a positive marriage you'll need to have a positive influence. Choose your influence carefully.

Bringing It Home

★ ★ ★

Strategy #7 for strengthening your marriage:

Work to overcome the undertows in your relationship.
Then work on becoming the best you in your relationship.

Questions to consider:

1. What hopes, dreams, desires and passions did you
   expect to have in your relationship?

   _____

   _____

   _____

   _____

   _____

2. Have these been met? If not, what can you do to meet
   these expectations?

   _____

   _____

   _____

   _____

   _____

3. How has deployment affected the strength of your relationship?

_____

_____

_____

_____

4. Have you considered marriage coaching as a means to gain / regain that strength? If not, why not?

_____

_____

_____

_____

5. Write down the vision for your marriage. Are you and your spouse in agreement with this vision? If not, consider getting some marriage coaching.

_____

_____

_____

_____

Final Thought: *Your marriage is what you make it.*

CHAPTER 8

Coming Home: Preparing on Both Fronts

"I knew the last couple weeks wouldn't go fast enough…"

Tonia wasn't sure whether or not to believe the news. After all, Mike's deployment had been postponed for months and she was certain his coming home was subject to the same delays. No sense blaming anyone for the delays. It is what it is – the price of being married to someone in the service, especially during times of conflict. Eighteen months. She never signed on board to be a military wife, not for a split second. That was the one thing she didn't want; the constant uncertainty, having her husband gone, raising the kids on her own, none of this appealed to her. No amount of patriotism would change this. But she adapted and it turned out her military experience was life changing – some of it good. At least she had a new appreciation for her relationship with her husband – when she could see through the moments of anger. Now with Mike coming home all she could do was keep busy – extremely busy. She didn't dare tell the kids dad's homecoming until he was stateside; then, and only then would she start telling the kids that dad would be home.

Tonia's experience with preparing for the homecoming is common. Anxiety, a rush of different emotions, and not too much hope for fear the plans might change. Then comes the feeling of apprehension of what life is going to be like together after they had been apart for so long. She had to be prepared mentally, everyday, for anything... good or bad. Routine was part of corporate life, not this life...and nothing seemed to be routine about her husband serving, except his being gone. And now that was changing.

For Mike, he took one day at a time. His reality was that any day could be his "home coming," just how he came home was the only differentiator. Now that he was pretty certain he'd be coming home alive (although there never really is any certainty until you reach the States), he was faced with thoughts of "Would he fit in, would people treat him kindly, would his children know who he is." When he left, his son was a baby who had yet to walk or talk; and since he had been away, his son had grown into a walking, talking toddler. How hard would it be to fit back into his life? What about his daughter? Would the transition back into her life be easy or uncomfortable? They'd written letters but sometimes he hid behind the pen. And Tonia, his wife, would she still love him if she knew everything he had to do during the war? Would he be able to open up emotionally to her – love her as she deserved to be loved?

There is so much emotion wrapped up in the homecoming. Mike and Tonia were the commanders of their own worlds, each making decisions that were vital to their day to day life. Brian and Jody were no different, despite Brian's short deployment. They faced the same questions Tonia and Mike faced. The only difference for Brian and Jody was their kids were older and they knew when dad was supposed to be home. Jody had to perform damage control when Brian's return home was delayed. *Why isn't dad home? You said he'd be home.* Just to bring humor to the situation, a friend sent a "WANTED" email to all of their friends humorously accusing Brian of violating the State's family abandonment code. Their friends laughed, but the children didn't get it.

Each couple seemed to face similar issues and struggled with what to do next. Along with all the excitement and anxiety of seeing each other, all the couples interviewed wondered how they were not only going to relate but how they were going to merge "commands." One marriage. Two different worlds.

From the Heart of a Child

Life at home was different from when Mike had left – even though Tonia had worked so hard to keep everything the same. The kids turned to her for everything and now she wondered whether they would eagerly embrace Mike and his influence or whether it would be an awkward transition. Sometimes it seemed like Mike being gone didn't matter to them; but she knew this was not the case and that his coming home would create a whirl wind of excitement. And change.

Tonia shared that she put her kids first; she protected them from any information that would cause them undue anxiety. As a result, she only had two weeks to prepare them – and herself – for Mike's homecoming. She had two young impressionable children to prepare and she had no idea how this change would influence them; or her for that matter. She had no idea really what to do. *Do we just pick up where we left off? What do we do? What do I do?* The parents with older children, like Jody and Cheryl, couldn't provide that same "protection" because their kids knew too much – they knew what was going on; but that didn't shed any ideas on what to do next.

Sometimes we can't see the immediate impact we have on our children, so we question everything we do as parents. As parents we run around making comments like "If we could only tap into the minds of our children and understand how they process the events and influences, then we could understand how they feel." Instead, we are typically placated by the child's token "I'm fine" answer.

Emily, age twelve, whose dad Larry was deployed right before he was to retire, put her thoughts to paper so others could understand the impact her dad's deployment had in her life. It provides a glimpse into the heart of a child; and from the heart of a child, we can learn that everything influences and everything matters, including coming home. From this you can prepare your children.

Sometimes

Sometimes I miss his hugs.

Sometimes I feel like he's never coming back to us.

Sometimes I wish he wasn't over there.

*Sometimes I eat Cheez-Its because he ate them in the
     video he sent us.*

Sometimes I cry because I miss him.

Sometimes I miss his nerdiness.

Sometimes I can't wait until July when he has leave.

*Sometimes I need help getting the lawnmower to start
     and he's not here.*

Sometimes he emails me.

Sometimes he sends my mom flowers; then she cries.

Sometimes my dog misses him.

*Sometimes my friends just assume that whenever I
     talk about him I'm going to bawl.*

Sometimes he calls.

*Sometimes on the phone, he says, 'I love you Emily.'
     And I say, 'I love you too, daddy.'*

*Sometimes people think he's in jail or something,
     but he's in Iraq.*

*Sometimes I don't have anybody's nails to do
     (he lets me massage his hands).*

Sometimes even Lily, my best friend, can't comfort me.

Sometimes I want him to come home.

Sometimes we eat junk for dinner.

Sometimes my Mom cries.

*Sometimes I realize life will be a whole lot better with
     my daddy home.*

Sometimes I realize life will be a whole lot better with my daddy home. The same goes if mom is the one coming home. Studies support that children do much better emotionally and academically when they have the influence of both mom and dad living happily together under one roof. The happily together part is key and it will take preparation and work. Your children will feed off your emotions as well as those of your spouse. Preparing your children has a lot to do with preparing yourself emotionally. Go back and re-read Emily's poem. Each sentence of Emily's poem is a glimpse of what she was thinking or feeling – it's a road map to the areas of her life where she hurt or had an emotional desire that needed to be comforted; and it also serves as a permission slip for you to take care of those same needs in your own children.

Preparing Your Soldier

On February 6, 2007 Jody sat down at her computer and typed out a check list of what Brian should expect upon his return. She had spent the last few days cleaning what seemed every nook and cranny of their home in preparation of his arrival and while she did this she had a few precious moments to think about Brian's homecoming. How could she make the transition easy for him? The whole sudden shock of civilian life might overwhelm him. After all, the kids were already bursting with excitement in anticipation of dad being home – would he be able to handle it? She just wanted everything to be perfect. She wanted her family to be the same as before Brian left. So she typed her list, which was intended to provide some much needed humor and tips:

Hello Darling,

Since we are getting down to you coming home, I thought I would get you ready for your arrival. Here are a few things you need to prepare and consider for your next mission (home).

1. Be ready for lots of wrestling. You already know this but I have to say it anyway. It is part of my job. Your children are really missing your physical contact.

2. Be ready to fit back into our lives. We live a totally different life than the military. We actually have a schedule that has children in it. We eat meals together, chat and yell, and cry together. We even have time for homework. A person coming in from the outside, especially a military person like yourself, would be led to believe it is total chaos; it is not. This is my job to remind you of our reality.

3. We are not soldiers. We are your family. We don't jump when someone yells a command. Even though mommy tries, I have found that I can shout commands all I want but I still have to be there standing over everything to make it happen. It is like teaching a class full of preschoolers who have no idea how to stay in the lines when coloring.

4. We have missed you so much that we will probably be in your face a lot. We have lots to talk about too. There may even be a lot of loud talk and every-one talking at once. Prepare yourself.

5. You may experience attitude from your chil-dren. You are a new authority figure coming in and helping mommy. They are used to Mommy and Mommy's ways.

6. Be prepared to share your bed. I like to cuddle. My feet are constantly cold.

7. Be prepared to share your space. You do not have a room by yourself anymore. There are five more people in your face, under your feet and at your side most of the time.

8. Be prepared to have things sometimes messy. We don't have maids here or anyone to do our laundry. You can always lend a hand whenever you see some-thing that needs to be picked up, cleaned or cooked.

9. Be prepared to wear normal clothes. We don't have uniforms in this establishment.

10. This place is not an alcohol free zone. We do drink wine on occasion. It is totally your choice to participate or not.

11. We attend church as a family. God is the center of our family and has provided for us above and beyond. We honor Him by going to church, praying together as a family, and talking about the wonder-ful things of God.

12. We do not use foul language. We try our best to use uplifting talk. Sometimes we fail, but we are human.

13. You will have your own vehicle. There are no chauffeurs here. You are required to transport yourself from one destination to the other.

14. We live on a farm that has twenty acres. You will be required to help with the animals, fencing, buildings, etc.

15. For the last five years we have coached a little league team. You are required to participate in this venture.

16. We live close to family members. You are required to see them. Not all the time, but we do get together for occasional gatherings in which your presence is required.

17. You are required to eat lunch with your children at least two times a year.

18. Be prepared to listen to your wife's nonsense talk. She is a wonderful woman and is required to use up to 25,000 words a day. She has been limited on this but will be making up for it upon your arrival. You have been chatting via instant messaging. You can't shut her off anymore.

19. Be prepared to give your wife time alone without the kids. Finding a sitter and delivering them to the grandparents has been a lot of work. You didn't have to do this. Also, be prepared to go out with your wife alone. You know, to a movie and dinner or just to walk around and be together.

20. Be prepared for lots of husband and wife time. The two of you haven't been together for awhile and you will need to make up for lost time. I'm sure baths are required as is massages and the like. It may be too much for you to handle, but knowing you, you'll rise to the occasion and be a good soldier.

I hope this list will help you in your upcoming mission. You may find it humorous as it was humorous to put together; but do realize it is reality as well. Keep this list on you at all times during your mission so that you will be able to go back to whatever you need help remembering...and remember, we love you!

Brian didn't find the humor in the list. Usually something like this would bring a smile to his face; instead, he felt his wife was telling him what to do. In his world, he did the "telling." In his short deployment, he was the one issuing the commands and controlling half a country and now his wife wanted to issue him orders for the next mission? Did she not think he could size up the mission of the family and make adjustments?

For Jody, the list was a great release sprinkled with humor and truth. Every point spoke to how she felt or was feeling. It was a window into her heart; it was her welcome home letter to Brian.

Despite the short time away, what was required of both to survive on each front changed the way they thought. Jody knew, after Brian's initial response to her letter, that there would be some much needed work on both their parts to unify their worlds.

So what can be done to better prepare the soldier and the spouse for the homecoming? Dr. Bridgett Cantrell, along with Vietnam veteran Chuck Dean co-authored the book *Down Range to Iraq and Back* that is quickly becoming a great resource for couples to read prior to the homecoming. In their book they offer answers, explanations and insights as to why so many combat vets suffer from flashbacks, depression, fits of rage and many other aspects of PTSD. Had Brian and Jody both read this book, perhaps Jody's letter would have been worded differently, or better yet, perhaps Brian would have responded better. Regardless, the letter is priceless because it speaks from the spouse to the soldier on so many levels.

Here are a few parting tips from Deputy Director Alfie Ramos, who also served in the active U.S. Army:

1. The process for readjustment should start prior to deployment by getting as much information as possible to make the absence and return more predictable.

2. There is nothing wrong with admitting that you need help in preparing for the homecoming. Check with

your VET Center regarding available family counseling or even individual counseling. The staff veterans will be able to relate and prepare you for what you can expect and give you ideas on how to prepare you and your spouse for the transition.

3. Speaking to the service member, you need to realize that your family expects "a return to normal" since the big stressors – deployment and enemy action – are about over. Life at home continued to move forward. Be prepared to ask for help.

4. Know that there is no such thing as "normal" and that upon return you both need to sit down as a family and talk about feelings and needs.

Just know that preparing your soldier has everything to do with preparing yourself if you are the spouse who was left behind.

The Homecoming Briefing

One of the many responsibilities Chaplain Alford had on base was to greet every soldier as they stepped off the plane and set foot back on U.S. soil. He knew that most soldiers had only one focus at this point: getting back into the arms of their loved ones. As Mike admitted, he and Tonia didn't really talk about the homecoming too much before his arrival because *literally until my plane left for Fort Bragg, I didn't think I was going to get out of Iraq.* So now that he had "made it" the only thing he could think about was getting home. Nothing else mattered.

Through trial and error, Chaplain Alford learned how to prepare the soldiers for the next two weeks of briefings they'd experience – he needed them to open their ears and hearts; he needed the next two weeks to matter and for the soldiers to gain understanding and give the process some attention before going home. If they would do this, then their transition back into their homes would be a bit easier. And so, the **14 Points of Acknowledgement** was born:

1. You do need this briefing.
2. You are not the same as when you left.
3. Your family is not the same as when you left.
4. Your community is not the same as when you left.
5. It will take time to readjust. (DO NOT get behind the wheel of a vehicle right away.)
6. It will take effort to readjust.
7. Some stress is normal.
8. What was unresolved before leaving is still unresolved.
9. Your expectations of reunion need to be tempered.
10. Everybody has a story.
11. You need to listen to your family's story.
12. Your family needs your praise.
13. There is help.
14. Not all the world is as ugly as what you have seen.

Chaplain Alford developed a system in which he speaks this information into the ear of the soldier and has them acknowledge each point after he speaks it. Though there is no sure-fire concrete evidence that this method works one hundred percent of the time, Chaplain Alford did state that his soldiers tend to pay attention more during the debriefing once he implemented this technique.

Over the course of many months, the military has recognized that certain symptoms take a while to surface. The excitement of the homecoming masks many dormant emotions. So, instead of rushing into mental health assessments upon return, where every soldier answers "fine," the soldiers will often participate in an assessment three to six months after their return. It is then that an evaluation takes place and direction for help is provided. This works great if your soldier is still with the Reserves or Guard and required to attend trainings once a month. If not, you both will need to take an active roll in seeking guidance and help.

The bottom line is to embrace the resources around you. Start with the VET Center or Military OneSource. Whatever you do, don't wait until you get into a mental abyss. If you've made the decision for better or for worse, then you should decide to do it happy.

Bringing It Home

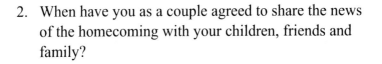

Strategy #8 for strengthening your marriage:

There is no such thing as "normal." Accept that you will have tough moments and that nothing is normal; but together, with help, you can make it.

Questions to consider:

1. What have you done to prepare for the homecoming mission?

    _____

    _____

    _____

    _____

2. When have you as a couple agreed to share the news of the homecoming with your children, friends and family?

    _____

    _____

    _____

    _____

3. Have you planned time as a couple to get reacquainted? If not, consider doing so.

_____

_____

_____

4. How do you plan to use the counseling resources made available to you and your spouse? As a tune-up or last resort?

_____

_____

_____

5. What will you do to encourage and empower your spouse and family through the homecoming?

_____

_____

_____

Final Thought: *Occasionally ask yourself 'would I want to be married to me.' If not, change to become that person you would want to be married to.*

CHAPTER 9

Living Life Together

"Deployment was hard but working through all the issues that war can leave on a soldier and family is honestly what is the hardest."

Jody was clearly frustrated. As she finished a bowl of berry cobbler, she shared how Brian just didn't "get it"; that his civilian life, in some ways, requires more of him than his military life did and he doesn't seem to embrace that. Brian attempted to interject but Jody continued...

They go over there with one job. Their job is this: they have their clothing decided for them, their food, when they sleep; their times to exercise...all they have to do is get up in the morning and do their job...

Jody's perception of Brian's reality was all she knew. He hadn't really opened up since he'd been home and she was only aware of some of the dangers Brian and the others faced from the emails he had shared. She wasn't discounting the fact that their job was often just to stay alive, but her reality was that she felt powerless. She just wanted to be the family they were before Brian left, and that seemed far from possible; she continued...

> *Then they come home – he was overwhelmed; Brian was way overwhelmed when he came back. He left what he did in civilian life (multiple jobs) behind to go to ONE job. He comes home and has all these other jobs...he was way overwhelmed...and not only that; he had to be a dad too!*

Reality without war; fighting perceptions of what you thought your spouse's reality was; having to face a new life yet one that is still burdened by those things that were left undone prior to leaving; not understanding your spouse's point of view...all this is pretty common. For both spouses.

It's for these reasons Steve Akers and other counselors and marriage coaches suggest service members and their families make the time to connect with someone in the counseling/coaching profession soon after the service member's return. The new reality – the whole idea of living life together for both spouses – can be overwhelming – to the point where you may feel you don't belong together. Mike and Tonia fought through these very issues. Mike fought through the idea of belonging to anywhere but the war zone.

New Reality

It's been a little more than two years since Mike returned from combat. Sometimes, as he and Tonia will admit, it seems like they are doing pretty good; that they are "going to make it." But then there are, as Tonia put it, *plenty of times when we feel like we are in an uphill battle and not getting anywhere.* Even with counseling, Mike still struggles to overcome some of the effects of war; and it's typically the small things that will set him down a destructive mental path...

> *One morning I was trying to cook breakfast and I put a plate on the warmer burner. I was trying to make this big breakfast and the plate just shattered....and....I just lost it. I'm like I don't belong here...I should be put...guys like me should just be put somewhere and brought out in times of war... because we don't belong in society. I didn't feel like I could do anything right – nothing felt right – part of me just wanted to go back over there. Because over there I knew what I was doing...it's like I almost felt more comfortable in war.*

Mike – and Brian – not only struggled with readjusting back into their homes, but dealing with their children. Jody shared that Brian struggled with having patience. In her words,

> *he has no patience whatsoever. You have to imagine – here's the Major, twenty guys in front of him... and what, now he has four children...but with these twenty guys it's "okay, here's what's going to happen, here's what we are going to do, blah, blah, blah"...so he talks to the kids this way. They*

have no clue...here's our second oldest looking at dad, thinking "screw dad, I'm not going to do this; what's going on over here?" Well hello, guess what happens? Mount St. Helens explodes and the kids go running for the hills.

Mike struggled with just the every day noise that kids make.

The noise from the kids was unnerving...I'm used to other things, bombings and guns...and then you've got this shrieking noise. Over there you are attuned to listening to every little thing and the noise from the kids and everything else just sets you off. You're listening to a crack...you're listening for anything (that would tip off where the enemy is)...and then you come home and its slam, bam, auuugh, kids screeching...

The feelings of being overwhelmed, not belonging and treating your family like soldiers are all very common. At the same time, you are fighting to keep your marriage together. Here's what you can do initially, according to counselors:

1. Agree as a couple to seek family counseling and even couples counseling so that everyone understands that this readjustment is going to take some work.

2. Come to terms with that fact that there is no shame in seeking help. It is important to believe that everyone needs a coach or mentor, especially during the challenging times.

Being proactive in the early stages of your readjustment will help you in a number of areas – with your children, your friendships and especially in your marriage relationship. Tonia mentioned that there is so much to overcome and work through…life together after war isn't easy, and keeping the marriage together – and happy – will likely be one of the hardest battles you fight.

Fighting to Keep the Marriage Together

Reality without war…or is it? No one is shooting at you, the family is balanced again and so life should be good. But everything – and as Jody stated, EVERYTHING – has changed. In some ways it's like the soldier never left the battlefield but yet physically he or she is home. The war is always there, regardless of where the soldier is physically. What you may have been accustomed to in your marriage prior to deployment is likely much different now. There's an uncomfortable and anxious feeling. Jody would look at Brian and see how UN-relaxed he was being home. Peter and Cheryl the same. For Peter, instead of engaging with his family, he'd find himself taking all day to do the front part of his little yard. Who knows the battles he was fighting in his little sanctuary.

The doubt and uncertainty of what you are doing in your relationship, whether you'll ever survive the changes, how'll you come to that point of being interdependent and not independent – all this puts pressure on your marriage relationship. As I mentioned in an earlier chapter, when I asked Mike and Tonia if it was a fight to keep their marriage together, her response was echoed by all the couples interviewed:

Fight is definitely the word I would use and have used. Deployment was hard but working through all the issues that war can leave on a soldier and family is honestly what is the hardest. I wanted so badly to be the family we were before Mike left, but unfortunately that was not the case and is not still. Mike had witnessed so much death, destruction and violence that it had left a lasting effect on him. There were times after his return that I really didn't think we were going to make it and that we would become a statistic of the Army; something I very much feared and still do. It is very hard not to take things personally when Mike is dealing with his issues and then there is the fact that I can't fix what is wrong. It took me a long time to get over the fact that I can try as hard as I want, but I can not make Mike better inside. The anger, flashbacks and unhappiness...all these are things he has to work out. I simply have to sit back and be there for him when he needs me.

Jody was fighting her own battles with Brian. Because Brian chose when he deployed, she had a hard time letting go of his decision and now that they were back together, the challenges they were facing were all because of his choice. As she clearly stated, *I didn't sign up to have a changed husband when he came home...and now I want some things taken care of.*

She wanted Brian to retire from the Reserves. Brian still wanted to make Lt. Colonel. One more issue causing friction instead of peace. And then the anger and flashbacks. Jody had no idea when Brian would fight the invisible enemy – one moment everything is good; the next moment there is anger or withdrawal. Life together after the war is often still a battle zone. Every day is a fight for both spouses. They share a mutual love, but often don't know how to show it or if it will be accepted.

Chaplain Griffith stated that is it absolutely crucial for couples to attend Strong Bonds or some form of marriage enrichment weekend that is offered by their branch, for those very reasons. These all expense paid weekend retreats are where the healing first begins in the marriage. It is important to attend a retreat as quickly as possible upon the return in order to provide the much needed reaffirmation of your love and commitment to each other. It will help you through some of the more difficult moments. When the marriage is right, it sets the foundation for all other relationships to be right. You'll have conflicts to work through, but every marriage has those to work through. The military programs are designed to compound the solutions to the point they overwhelm the problem. Your marriage will look different, no doubt; but if you are proactive, you'll come out stronger. Get good at loving and respecting each other and you'll resolve conflicts much quicker.

Resolving Conflicts

There are numerous books available that suggest how to resolve conflict. Terry Felber, who is an international speaker, missionary, author of several books and a successful business owner mapped out a credible guideline for resolving conflict. He starts where we all should start, on what NOT to do:

1. Avoiding conflict doesn't resolve anything. Talk about the issue.
2. Silent Treatment. The mind is very powerful...silence without solution only causes problems.
3. Tortuous Nagging. Need I say more?
4. Power Plays. The "if you don't give me what I want, I won't give you what you want" scenario is not a good solution. Men typically withhold money and women typically withhold sex in the relationship.
5. Blame Game.
6. Complaining to other people about the person you have the disagreement with.

Constructive Resolutions

1. Understand that nothing is a big deal – everything can be worked through.
2. Forgive and forget past indiscretions.
3. De-personalize everything. Deal with the issue or conflict and not the person. (Granted, this is definitely easier said than done.)
4. Ask for forgiveness.
5. Stay proactive. Maintain low tones when you are discussing disagreements; the goal is to resolve the issue and not react to the person.

6. Never discuss anything after 9:00PM; unless you are willing to commit to resolving the issue before you go to bed. Bottom line: don't go to bed angry.

7. Never discuss anything of potential conflict over the phone. The same goes with email. Body language and facial expressions are often vital in understanding meaning or intent. This can't be conveyed properly through the phone or email.

Keeping your marriage strong has nothing to do with circumstances and everything to do with commitment.

Decide and Commit

Regardless of the struggles, all the couples interviewed had made the decision to stay married. They probably didn't think readjustment would be that tough; but they quickly came to the conclusion that starting over wouldn't be easier. They stayed committed to their decision.

The couples interviewed started the deployment journey with relatively healthy relationships free of alcohol or spousal abuse issues. They had history and memories to pull them through some of the difficult moments and often chose to channel their anger and difficult moments into remembering that history.

If you are newly married, it is even more important that you remember why you married in the first place. You won't have a whole lot of history to fall back on so you have to cast a vision for what you want your married life to look like and then pursue it with a passion together; and it will be difficult, especially when you are dealing with all the readjustment issues.

Here's the secret: you will have to hold on to the belief that your greatest joy in life will come through your loving relationships. You also have to believe that your marriage is more than what it is right now. Your marriage should always be in the "becoming" state: becoming great, becoming better; if you've "arrived" in your marriage, your marriage is not growing and that is when new challenges arise.

So, decide and commit. Work through the issues together, seek counseling and absolutely know that you can make it. Others have successfully gone before you so there is no reason why you can't make it with commitment and hard work.

What about Tonia and Mike, Jody and Brian, Cheryl and Peter, and the others? They continue to work at their marriages every day. They're going to counseling and they're learning how to relate again. They're learning that it is okay to be vulnerable in a trusting relationship because that builds trust and says you are trusting. They love each other unconditionally and yet there are still days they want to kill each other...so, they are slowly but surely getting back to "normal." Whatever that is.

Tear this page out if you need to and post it on your mirror so you have a road map from which to guide your marriage:

DECIDE that:

D – Divorce will not solve most of my problems.

E – Everyone has a story to tell and deserves to be heard. Listen to what my spouse has to share.

C – Commitment is core to my marriage. Let my spouse know that I am committed to us.

I – Integrity matters.

D – Defending my marriage from negative influence or from speaking negatively about it is a worthy fight.

E – Encouragement is healthier than criticism for my marriage.

COMMIT to being:

C – Counseled by someone who has the marriage I want, if I am unhappy.

O – Open and honest with my spouse.

M – Mature in my conversations. The goal is to deal with the issues and not make it personal.

M – Mentored in areas where I am weak or uncomfortable in my marriage.

I – Intimate in my relationship. Be romantic; date my spouse and find ways to connect not only physically but emotionally.

T – Teachable. Apply what I have read and what others who have gone before me have shared that will strengthen my marriage.

There's an old cliché that says anything worthwhile in your life you will have to fight for. This is true even more so today. Our freedom, our beliefs, the principles from which this country was born…and especially our marriages require our commitment and a willingness to fight for their preservation. What we do today does affect generations. How we treat our marriages does influence our children and the strength of our country.

Together, as a family, you have served our country well. Thank you. Now serve your family – both of you. Living your life together can be as you imagined when you first got married.

Bringing It Home

★ ★ ★

Strategy #9 for strengthening your marriage:

Your marriage is ordained, whether by God or by fate so decide and commit to your original marriage vision. Your mission is to strengthen your marriage so ask for help if you need it.

Final Thought: *Strong marriages plus strong families does equal a strong military. Stay focused on strengthening your marriage and as a result we will continue to have a strong nation.*

About the Author

Michael Schindler spent the early part of his childhood growing up on Elmendorf Air Force Base where his dad was employed by the Alaskan Air Command as an engineer. His dad later transferred to the Army Corp of Engineers and Mike spent the next fifteen years under the continued influence of men and women in uniform.

Michael enlisted in the US Navy where he experienced the culture of Singapore, Japan, Philippines, and parts of Malaysia. Through his personal experiences in the military and his exposure to the hardships of long deployments on servicemen and women and their families, Mike began to see firsthand the need for marriage support services.

Years later, those experiences led Michael to found Operation Military Family – an organization committed to developing sound strategies designed to strengthen military families.

As an inspirational speaker and trainer he is a strong advocate and promoter of what our government and our military is doing "right" because, as he is known to say, "The media does a great job of pointing out what isn't going so right." His message of Strong Marriages equal Strong Families equal Strong Servicemen and Women continues to gain momentum throughout all the military branches. This is especially true during the current level of high deployment tempo.

Michael is a graduate of Western Washington University and continues to serve as CEO of a web-based franchising firm in addition to his commitment to Operation Military Family. He and his wife, Keri, currently reside in Edmonds, Washington with their two daughters, Taylor and Reilley.